THE BUSINESSMAN'S GUIDE TO

Advertising & Sales Promotion

HERSCHELL GORDON LEWIS
Chairman, Lewis/Nelson/Kahn, Inc.
Chicago, Illinois

Gregg and Community College Division
McGraw-Hill Book Company

New York/St. Louis/Dallas/San Francisco/Düsseldorf
Johannesburg/Kuala Lumpur/London/Mexico/Montreal
New Delhi/Panama/Paris/São Paulo/Singapore/Sydney
Tokyo/Toronto

This book was set in Theme by Creative Book Services, a division of McGregor & Werner, Incorporated. The designer was Creative Book Services. The cover designer was Charles Carson.

Library of Congress Cataloging in Publication Data

Lewis, Herschell Gordon, date.
    The businessman's guide to advertising and sales
promotion.

    1. Advertising.   2. Sales promotion.   I. Title.
HF5823.L643   659.1   73-20325
ISBN 0-07-037526-7

1 2 3 4 5 6 7 8 9 MUMU 7 3 2 1 0 9 8 7 6 5 4

PREFACE

This isn't just another book about advertising.

For some years, I've not only taught courses and given lectures on the principles of advertising and sales promotion but also practiced these principles every day for clients whose budgets don't run into the millions.

As a teacher, I have found that most existing texts are not relevant. They present theory instead of fact, and the typical advertising student, who is trying to learn something that will help him do more business, is frustrated by examples that are not directly related to his needs. As the head of a medium-sized advertising agency, I similarly have found that examples and statistics in most textbooks too often pertain only to giant advertisers.

What about the businessman taking advertising as an evening course who wants specific information that will help him tomorrow? What about the student who doesn't want a history or a collection of famous ads, but who wants a book that will give him practical assistance?

These are the people for whom I wrote *The Businessman's Guide to Advertising and Sales Promotion*. In this book I've tried to minimize abstract theory and maximize hard fact, to use examples that make sense to businessmen and students alike, and to codify the principles of effective advertising in a comprehensible manner.

A few of my personal prejudices toward advertising may appear in this text: I object to trickiness, to the use of mechanical effects to cover up a lack of imagination, and to the masking of simple rules with high-flown terminology.

This, therefore, is a straightforward "how to" book. It is also a book that grapples with the problems faced by today's businessman. Instant communications, future shock, and consumerism have dictated new approaches to advertising and sales promotion. *The Businessman's Guide* to *Advertising and Sales Promotion* is a guide to survival for today's advertiser.

ORGANIZATION

The text is organized into six chapters, each of which develops a major topic.

Chapter 1, "Reaching and Influencing People," explores the functions of advertising and sales promotion. The chapter examines the different kinds of advertising media and sales promotion methods available to businessmen.

Chapter 2, "Words That Sell," discusses the effective use of words in advertisements. Special emphasis is given to writing headlines and body copy.

Chapter 3, "Designing the Printed Ad," deals with layout, graphics, and printing. The production of newspaper advertising is stressed, since this medium is the most widely used by small- and medium-sized businesses.

Chapter 4, "Direct Mail and the Broadcast Media," covers these media in depth and includes guidelines on when and how to use them most effectively.

Chapter 5, "Sales Promotion Methods," explains the distinction between publicity and public relations and tells how to use each successfully. Displays and exhibits are also covered in this chapter.

Chapter 6, "Planning and Evaluation," tells businessmen where they can get professional help and how to evaluate it. It also introduces students to market research and describes methods of budgeting advertising and sales promotion. The book ends with a discussion of future trends in the field.

Each chapter contains activities designed to provide maximum student involvement. These activities can be individualized to suit the particular needs of each student.

An instructor's manual and key is also available to teachers using the text. It contains specific teaching suggestions for each chapter and suggested answers for the end-of-chapter activities. In addition, it provides a reference bibliography and a ready-to-duplicate final exam.

ACKNOWLEDGMENTS

The writer of any book is indebted to others for their inspiration. Most notable in this instance is David Ogilvy, whose *Confessions of an Advertising Man* marked the beginning of the process of codifying advertising rules (which this book hopefully completes).

I am also indebted to my advertising students at Roosevelt University, Chicago, Illinois, and to those who have attended my professional seminars at the University of Illinois; these groups have helped refine and update the material in this book. My office staff, surely the most efficient and loyal ever assembled, have singly and collectively, made so many contributions that I could never enumerate them. My special thanks go to Charlotte West, who obtained many of the exhibits and statistics presented in this text.

And to my wife Helene, who is not only the most thorough proofreader I know but also the best public relations expert, I give my thanks—for her help in those areas and for her help in keeping me on the right side of sanity.

Herschell Gordon Lewis

CONTENTS

CHAPTER ONE

Reaching and Influencing People

How do I sell it? Yesterday's businessman could gauge the salability of his product or the demand for his service by asking himself three questions about it: "Do they want it?" "Is the price right?" "Do they know about it?" If he could answer "yes" to each question, he also could assume that he'd do business.

The clever businessman, however, didn't leave those answers completely to chance. Part of his job was to create the selling climate—to see to it that people wanted his product or service, thought the price was right, and knew about it. He was aware that word of mouth was too slow a process of sales promotion to satisfy his selling needs.

Today's businessman, also, knows that a selling climate seldom develops accidentally or automatically. It must be generated, and he must be the generator:

- "Do they want it?" They will want it, if a carefully mounted advertising and sales promotion campaign tells them why they should have it.

- "Is the price right?" It will be accepted as right, if the value of the product is explained in terms that make sense to the buyer.

- "Do they know about it?" They will know about it, if the campaign fulfills the basic function of any intelligent advertising: to reach, at the lowest possible cost, the most people who can and will buy what one has to sell.

When a businessman talks about advertising and sales promotion, he should not think of these facets of marketing as strange arts practiced by sorcerers or charlatans. That so many businessmen do think in these terms indicates a widespread misunderstanding of the principles of communications. It also reveals a basic misconception of the role of advertising and sales promotion in moving goods from the producer to the consumer.

FUNCTIONS OF ADVERTISING AND SALES PROMOTION

There is much overlap between the functions of advertising and sales promotion. Some people consider all efforts to encourage sales as "sales promotion" and thereby include advertising as a form of sales promotion. Others refer to advertising as "any paid form of nonpersonal promotion of goods or services by an identified sponsor" and to sales promotion as "those activities that supplement both personal selling and advertising." It is in this latter sense that the terms are used in this manual.

Sometimes one plus one can equal three or five or eight. This is called "synergism." *Synergism* occurs when the total effect is greater than the sum of the effects of its individual parts. Advertising and sales promotion are synergistic worlds, for often the total effect of a campaign is much greater than the sum of the effects of its individual parts.

Confusing? Think of it this way: Repetition builds up an increasing impact on the consciousness and memory of the prospective customer. A single ad stressing a theme might be remembered for a single day. Two ads with the same theme might be remembered for three days. Ten ads stressing the same theme might cause that theme to be remembered for 100 days.

The slogans, phrases, and jingles of advertising, which usually are the forms in which themes are expressed, stay with us, not necessarily because they are memorable but because they are repeated. Today, in the 1970s, many people can recall with total accuracy slogans, phrases, and jingles that have not been heard since World War II. Because they were used repeatedly before and during World War II, they became etched on the memory. Almost every adult over forty can still hum the five-note Jell-O jingle that was associated with Jack Benny's popular radio program, and most of them would connect the line, "Ask the man who owns one," with Packard cars, although they haven't been manufactured for years.

A good theme, then, and a careful choice of methods to produce the maximum impact: these are the basic elements of a potent advertising and sales promotion campaign.

But regardless of the theme chosen and regardless of the exact methods decided upon, all advertising and sales promotion should be designed to accomplish one or both of these two basic goals: to generate sales and to create and maintain an image.

Generating Sales

Which detergent is best? Which margarine? Which toothpaste? Research indicates that although the consumer's primary concern in choosing a brand is price, the next most important reason why consumers choose one brand rather than another is advertising. When faced with a choice between brands, the consumer tends to reach for the one that seems most familiar—usually the brand whose advertising has made the greatest impact on his memory.

A careful businessman knows what percentage of the market he now commands. He should also know what and where his potential market is. His immediate challenge is to maintain his present share of the market; his long-range challenge is to increase that share if possible. Whether he wants simply to hold his present share of business or whether he is determined to add to his share, advertising and sales promotion are the obvious and logical ways to generate the sales he needs.

Advertising and sales promotion work to generate sales in the following ways:

- They support and reinforce the salesman in the field. In general, any salesman whose product is known to the prospective customer or retailer because of an extensive consumer advertising and sales promotion campaign has had part of his selling job done for him.

- They reach prospective customers inaccessible by any other means. Any use of mass media contacts hundreds, thousands, or millions more prospective customers than an individual salesman possibly could contact, and often an ad will be read, or a brochure studied, or a window display admired by someone who would refuse to listen to a personal sales presentation.

- They make product knowledge available quickly. When a businessman releases an improved product or service he can give every potential customer full details within a matter of days by using advertising and sales promotion techniques; a retailer with a special offering for his customers can use similar methods to get the news to them, sometimes even within a matter of hours.

- They open new lines of distribution. Not only do advertising and sales promotion encourage repeat sales to regular customers; they also are the most important weapons the businessman has for winning new customers.

- They reduce the cost of selling the product by increasing the number of sales made. In general, the per-unit cost of a product tends to decrease as the number of units sold increases. Thus an advertising and sales promotion campaign can be a way of spending money to save money (as well as to make money).

The Company Size Doesn't Matter.   How the giants in the business world handle their multimedia campaigns is obvious to anyone who reads the ads in the newspapers, listens to the radio, watches television, or looks through the brochures in his mail. When a major company launches an important campaign to generate sales, the theme of that campaign soon seems to be nearly everywhere. But even a small company can use similar techniques to generate sales. Its budget and use of techniques will be more modest, but the effect on those at whom the campaign is aimed can be equally powerful.

Consider, for example, a small manufacturer of a specific type of toy. Since it is a small company with limited money available for advertising and sales promotion, it cannot consider the kind of coast-to-coast television advertising schedule placed by the major toy manufacturers. Yet the small company could use a reduced version of the same technique to generate sales on a city-by-city basis.

The company might work up a single television commercial, together with a few newspaper ads and point-of-purchase material consistent with the chosen theme of the campaign. The company might then choose one or two cities, offering to key retail outlets in those cities a stock of the toy based on the forthcoming promotional push in that market. Today's retailers know that this approach to marketing does work, and this knowledge might well convince them to participate in the promotion of the toy. Thus, within one specific market, the small manufacturer has duplicated the approach of the giant manufacturer.

Armed, it is hoped, with a success story from this first marketing activity, the company chooses additional markets, repeating the procedure and refining it as experience brings a greater knowledge of which approach succeeds and which one is less effective.

Obviously, therefore, a businessman's share of his market is tied to his advertising and sales promotion campaign.

The Product Does Matter.   No advertising and sales promotion campaign, no matter how it is put together, can work miracles for a product or a service that is so inferior or so unattractive or so wrong in one way or another that no market for it exists. All a campaign can do is to give exposure to a product; then, if that product has a legitimate market, that exposure will generate the sales. If a consistent, clever, creative advertising and sales promotion campaign brings a momentary surge of sales, and then sales slump again, it is the product that is deficient, not the campaign. If the product does not satisfy the customer, no campaign can keep sales rising.

It also can happen that a product is satisfactory in itself but is being offered to the wrong market. Imagine, for instance, that a campaign for a brewery generated some additional sales, but then the sales level began slipping again. The campaign was good; the budget was adequate—but the product simply wasn't the right one for the area. The brewery was trying to generate extra sales for a dark, heavy beer in a market that preferred a pale, light beer. To get the added sales the brewery wants, the promotional effort would have to be shifted to a brew that might satisfy the tastes of the particular market area—or the brewery might try a campaign that combines education with promotion, in an attempt to teach the beer drinkers of the area to "Enjoy the true taste of old-world richness!"

Creating and Maintaining an Image

A druggist says, "I don't get it. This aspirin is identical to that one, and yet I sell more of that one at 69 cents a bottle than I do of this one at 49 cents a bottle." The two bottles of aspirin may be identical to the druggist, but they obviously are different in the eyes of the customers. The difference is probably one of image. The more expensive aspirin probably has an image that means "safety, quality, dependability" to its customers. In spite of the difference in price, and in spite of their being medically identical, that image, intangible as it is, will strengthen the sales of the more expensive brand. And this is proof that image is sometimes as important as the product itself. In marketing, what the prospective customer thinks of the product is the reason for success—or lack of it.

"Image" is a big word in advertising and sales promotion today. *Image* is the opinion that the customer has, an opinion that has been influenced by each contact the customer has had with a product and a company.

What the Right Image Is. A good image, the right image, will help a businessman find the customers he needs, and it will encourage those customers to buy from him. A bad or even simply a misleading image can cripple and sometimes kill a marketing operation.

What constitutes a good image, the right image, may be quite different for one company, product, or service than for another. A small women's specialty store, for instance, may want to project an image that says "exclusive, top quality, designer models, one of a kind, personal service" to its particular group of customers. A mass merchandiser, on the other hand, may want to project an image that "bargains, large variety, dependability, easy self-service shopping" are available to its customers.

Image can be as important as price because it can predetermine quality. The image of a company, a product, or a service tells the customer what type of value/product to expect. For example, the high-fashion houses of Paris base their price structure not on the fabric in their garments but

Courtesy of Busch's Jewelry Co., New York, N.Y.

This ad projects the image of a jewelry store which will appeal to the budget-minded shopper.

rather on the image of the label. These merchandisers have spent years building an image that enables them to justify a charge for the value of the label that may be far in excess of the value of the product itself. Thus, image is not only a commentary on the product or business; it might be thought of as part of the product or business.

To understand this point, one need only recognize that anything that is marketed is, in the mind of the buyer, what it is PLUS what that buyer believes it is. Because of this, one insurance company may command more business than another whose rates are lower; one antifreeze with chemical content identical to another will sell twice as much as the second brand; one beauty parlor can charge twice as much for a hairset as its competitor.

A marketer should remember that it is what his customers expect, not what he himself wants, that determines his proper image. He must be sure that the image he projects reflects the type of operation the majority of his customers want. If a marketer decides to change his image, then he must be prepared to lose old customers to whom the new image will not appeal, and he must be sure that he can attract a sufficient number of new customers to make up for this loss.

Courtesy of Tiffany & Co.

The store emphasizing an aristocratic image can whisper price rather than shout it.

How Image Is Projected. Image is influenced by every contact a customer has with a product or a company; obviously, advertising and sales promotion are among the most important tools used to create and maintain the right image. Advertising is the most important nonpersonal link between the marketer and his customer.

Every element of a promotional campaign, therefore, should be designed with the proper image in mind and should be planned to help strengthen that image. This applies to advertising, promotional mailings, displays—every tool that an advertising and sales promotion campaign might use.

In order to strengthen the particular image it wishes to project, a specialty store might run a regular schedule of high-fashion ads (perhaps just an artist's sketch of a new style, the designer's name, and the store's name and address) in a local newspaper and in regional editions of fashion magazines. A mass merchandiser, however, might put his money into full-page ads in a local newspaper—each ad packed with lists of items, emphasizing prices—and into throwaway sheets and direct mail enclosures of the same type. Both companies would be advertising similar products, but each would be using advertising to strengthen a particular image that it wishes to project.

ADVERTISING MEDIA

The most effective advertising medium is that which reaches, at the lowest possible cost, the most people who can and will buy what a marketer is selling.

This approach suggests that a high-priced product, such as a Rolls-Royce automobile, might well find that *The New Yorker,* even though the cost per reader is higher, is a better media buy than *Parents' Magazine.* Why? Because research probably would show that *The New Yorker* readers, on the average, are in a higher income group than are readers of *Parents' Magazine.* In the same way, the exclusive store may choose media that reach mostly higher-income neighborhoods, while the store catering to the budget buyer may select media that reach mostly middle- and lower-income neighborhoods.

The definition of what constitutes effective advertising emphasizes reaching and influencing not just those who can buy but also those who

WILL buy. Sometimes the two groups are identical: those who will buy, who have a want or a need for the product, are a smaller group within the group of those who can buy.

Occasionally, those who will buy, those who have a want or a need for the product, do not actually have the ability to buy but can cause that purchase to be made. That is why toy manufacturers, baking companies, and many food processors concentrate their television advertising in the hours when children are likely to be watching. While the children themselves seldom can make the purchase, they can force the purchase to be made.

The choice of media is no simple task. As the channels of communication themselves become more numerous, the job of media selection inevitably becomes more specialized.

A hundred years ago, advertising was a far less complex problem. Only two basic media were available: newspapers and magazines. Point-of-purchase display was the only sales promotion method used. Both advertising and sales promotion, in those days, were used primarily as announcements rather than as tools of salesmanship. Goods were less plentiful; outlets were less numerous—and competition, therefore, was far less intense. In those days, an announcement of the availability of a product usually was sufficient to attract customers.

Today, competition is far more intense, and advertising has become much more complex. There are many media available to the advertiser, each carrying its own advantages and disadvantages.

The most commonly used media are the print media, which include newspapers and magazines, and the broadcast media, which include radio and television. Direct mail is also an important form of advertising as are outdoor and transit advertising. And there is a wide range of more specialized and exotic media, known as specialty advertising, which include everything from telegrams to skywriting.

Media fall into two categories: mass and selective. *Mass media* are those that reach the greatest number of people, with little regard for ethnic, economic, or social guidelines. Metropolitan newspapers are a mass medium: they circulate to everyone within their geographic limits, and their readers include the very rich, the very poor; those who live in the center of the city, those who live in the suburbs; workers; tradesmen; young people, old people. Lack of specific reader breakdown makes newspapers a mass medium. However, individual sections of a newspaper may be selective: an advertiser may specify that he wants his advertisement in the business, sports, women's, or amusement section. Foreign-language newspapers are also a selective medium.

Selective media are those that reach a particular social, economic, or special-interest group. Such a group may have as its common denominator an interest in sports; the same professional background or a common trade; a similarity of religious or national background; or an interest in the arts, or in medicine, or in economic commentary, or in travel—or the group may simply be men or women or children. Any medium that caters to a group bound by any one common field of interest can be said to be selective.

Broadcast media can be mass or selective. A typical family-oriented station will broadcast programming with a general appeal, to all types of listeners, during the morning rush hours. Daytime programming becomes mildly selective, aimed at one group—the housewives. Early evening programming, heard by the entire family, again is mass-oriented. And, often, late evening programming, with sports news and commentary, is again mildly selective, aimed at a masculine audience.

Some stations are selective throughout their broadcast day, as will be discussed later in this chapter.

Magazines generally are regarded as a selective medium. One reason is that the income level of magazine readers is universally higher than that of newspaper readers. Some magazines take pains to determine the selectivity of their readership. And, of course, all business publications are selective, since they reach special-interest groups.

Some advertisers add another category: the "speculative" media. *Speculative media* are not a parallel category to mass or selective media; rather they are media that normally would not be considered for the advertising of a particular product or service; for this reason, there is less competitive advertising in them. A simple example is media selection for a women's product, which usually would be advertised in publications catering to women or on broadcast stations at hours when the audience is primarily female. Speculatively, the advertiser may decide to experiment by advertising in men's publications, with the emphasis shifted to gift suggestion. Or he may try to broaden the base by appealing to teen-age girls. Any such type of advertising would change the media from selective to speculative. Thus, there are no particular speculative media as there are particular mass or selective media; any medium can be speculative. A medium becomes speculative only through its relationship to a particular marketing problem.

On a competitive basis, each advertising medium has its own advantages and disadvantages. Let us explore the most important of these.

Newspaper Advertising

Traditionally, newspapers have been accepted as the most potent advertising medium at the retail level. Broadcast media are becoming increasingly effective, and time salesmen from radio and television stations claim that their audiences entitle them to prime consideration from local retail advertisers. However, most retailers still believe that newspapers are a better buy.

This preference reflects logic as well as tradition. Many a housewife who travels to the store with the torn-out copy of an ad or a coupon in her handbag would be unable to respond in the same way were she forced to rely on broadcast media. Direct mail may offer the same advantage, but it is slow and expensive in comparison to the newspaper advertisement.

This referral factor is important. Visualize a store with a sale of men's furnishings, offering:

Suits with two pairs of pants	$85.00
Permanent press shirts, two for	8.00
Neckties	.99
Raincoats	15.00

And now, without looking at the list again, quote those prices. Even though you just read them, you may not recall all of them. However, you can look back to check them. This ability to look back and check is the *referral factor*, which is an important advantage of newspaper advertising. Because of the referral factor, the newspaper advertisement is an excellent way to give detailed information about a multiplicity of items, sizes, fabrics, prices, and descriptions. It also is an excellent way to give mail-order information and to present the shopper with a coupon. The referral factor, for instance, is why supermarkets, late each week, run full-page newspaper ads jammed with item listings, prices, and coupons.

Newspaper ads offer the advantage of the referral factor; that is, they enable the buyer to study details and to look back and check them.

The housewife preparing to do her weekend food shopping studies these ads carefully, comparing prices and offerings, looking both for menu suggestions and for ways to stay within her food budget.

The newspaper offers an advertiser a minimum lapse between the time an ad is prepared and the time it appears. This is very important to the retailer whose daily inventory level can determine what he wants to emphasize in his ads. The newspaper also offers the advertiser a maximum of space variations, for he can run a few inches one day and take a full page or even supply an entire preprinted supplement another day.

Finally, being somewhat departmentalized, a newspaper can encourage reading of the ads by placing those ads adjacent to editorial material that mirrors the interests of those most likely to be prospective customers. Advertisements aimed specifically at men can be placed on sports and financial pages. Advertisements aimed at women can be placed near fashion news.

In addition to the daily newspapers common to every metropolitan area, there are three other types of newspapers usually available to the advertiser: shoppers' guides, community newspapers, and the ethnic press.

Shoppers' Guides. In the period immediately preceding World War II, a number of newspapers designated as "shoppers' guides" grew up, but almost all of them died by around 1950. In the 1970s, however, using brighter formats and, often, magazine sizes, they are enjoying a noteworthy renaissance.

Shoppers' guides consist almost completely of advertising placed by local advertisers. The typical shoppers' guide is published weekly or monthly. Usually it is distributed free, although those that limit themselves to classified ads sometimes charge for copies distributed.

Readership of these publications is remarkably high, reinforcing newspaper publishers' contention that people read newspapers as much for advertising information as they do for news. A disadvantage of some of these publications is their infrequency of publication. The advertiser who must plan his promotions far in advance does not enjoy the flexibility that the advertiser in daily newspapers can anticipate.

Community Newspapers. Each suburb of any large city, and many sections of the city itself, may be served by one, two, or even three community newspapers. These papers limit themselves to news and features about the immediate locality.

Most community newspapers are published weekly, but an increasing number are published twice a week and some of the more important ones are issued daily. The weeklies often select Thursday as the optimum publishing day, since Friday and Saturday are the big shopping days. The twice-a-week community papers usually choose Monday and Thursday as publication days, with the Monday edition usually lagging behind the Thursday edition in its ability to gain advertising and readership.

Readership of these publications within the community is usually high and thorough. These newspapers offer the small, local retailer an excellent and inexpensive way to reach a pinpointed audience. For the regional or national advertiser, however, mounting a regional or national consumer campaign through community newspapers can be ponderous, tortuous, expensive, and inexact.

Ethnic Press. There are some powerful newspapers serving ethnic elements within a community. Within a single urban market, there may be daily or weekly newspapers in Spanish, German, Polish, Hebrew, Italian, and Chinese. Occasionally there will be two or even three newspapers serving a single foreign-language group within a large metropolitan area.

Because of the decline in immigration, foreign-language newspapers are less powerful than they once were. Nevertheless, there still are many older people, some with substantial buying power, who read no newspaper other than their foreign-language paper, and others who read it as a second paper. In some cities, recent Spanish-speaking immigrants—primarily from Puerto Rico—ensure the ethnic press serving this group of a readership for years to come.

Foreign-language newspapers accept as a matter of course their obligation to translate submitted advertising into the proper idiom. Almost without exception, these translations are accurate and literate. These papers offer a unique way of reaching a carefully delineated group of customers, but that same delineation, which involves the age, tastes, and background of a reader who may be atypical of the reader of conventional metropolitan newspapers, makes these papers an unlikely medium for many kinds of advertising.

In almost every metropolitan market, there are newspapers supported

Many advertisers in ethnic publications adapt the illustration (and often the copy) to match the readership of such publications.

Courtesy of PepsiCo, Inc.

by the black community. Although these newspapers are usually supplemental reading—for their readers usually read one of the metropolitan dailies as well—some of them have an extensive circulation and strength. Most are weeklies; a few are dailies.

In considering whether to purchase space in the ethnic press, the care that must be exercised is simply the same care that should underlie all selective media purchases: the businessman should ask himself, "Is the readership one that can and will buy what I have to sell?"

Magazines

Magazines generally are divided into two groups: consumer magazines and trade magazines. *Consumer magazines* are those read by the general public. They may appeal to a particular segment of the population or may concentrate on a particular subject, but so long as their specialty is not business-oriented, the publication is considered a consumer magazine. For instance, religious magazines, sports magazines, and travel magazines are all considered consumer magazines. *Trade magazines*, on the other hand, are those publications with a business-related readership. They are circulated to readers within a particular industry, trade, or profession, and their subject matter concerns that particular industry, trade, or profession. For instance, magazines intended for doctors, retailers, or transportation executives are trade magazines. Farm magazines are not quite consumer publications and not quite trade publications; Standard Rate and Data Service includes them as a separate category of consumer publications.

Advertising in magazines offers three unique advantages. First, no existing type of advertising has greater longevity than magazine advertising. A magazine may be read and saved by one person for a week or a month. It may also be passed from hand to hand, being read by a number of people over an extended period of time. As long as that magazine continues to be read, its advertising remains "alive."

Second, at present no other form of advertising enables a businessman to show his wares with better fidelity and quality than a magazine. The reproduction of artwork and photographs is much better in a well-printed magazine than in even the best-quality newspaper. In fact, many of the printing processes that make this possible were developed specifically for advertising use. Although television can show the product in action, the picture is less detailed and is transitory, and with television there is no referral factor. The only possible competitor for reproduction quality could be direct mail, which is a considerably more expensive medium.

Third, magazine advertising tends to carry with it the same prestige that the publication itself has. For instance, stores sometimes use a display of fashions with a sign, "as advertised in *Vogue*," or "as advertised in *Harper's Bazaar*," believing—correctly—that the prestige of the magazine adds to the sales appeal of the product. In addition, quality magazines of both consumer and trade categories tend to command strong reader loyalty, and readers extend this loyalty to the products advertised in those magazines.

Another advantage of advertising in magazines is that magazine advertising readership is increasing each year, perhaps because of the increase in the amount of leisure time. A 1971 research report showed that over a 10-year period, readership of magazine advertising had risen dramatically. For example, a typical full-color one page advertisement, noted by 29 percent of the readers of a mass-circulation magazine during the year

1959-1960, had risen to 39 percent 10 years later. A typical black-and-white full-page advertisement, noted by 19 percent during 1959-1960, was noted by 29 percent 10 years later.[1]

One disadvantage of magazine advertising for retailers is the infrequency of publication. Monthly magazines are impractical for retailers, since closing dates, or advertising deadlines, are far ahead. Even weekly magazines cannot compete with the short closing dates of newspapers.

Weeklies Versus Monthlies.   According to reader research, an average copy of a monthly magazine tends to be read by more readers than an average copy of a weekly magazine. Someone who hasn't read one week's copy of a weekly may toss it out unread when the next week's copy arrives, whereas each copy of a monthly tends to stay "alive" for at least a month. For this reason, advertising in monthly magazines may reach more readers per dollar than advertising in weekly magazines.

On the other hand, weeklies have strong advantages. They have a timeliness that makes them likely to be read before a monthly magazine. They are more likely to generate a regular reading pattern. Weeklies also offer the advertiser a shorter lapse between the time his ad must be ready and the time it appears. A weekly's advertising deadline may be one to four weeks in advance of publication, while a monthly's advertising deadline may be one to three months in advance of publication.

The trend is towards an increase in the frequency of issues. First, more frequent publication offers a magazine more opportunity for advertising revenue. Because a weekly magazine publishes 52 issues a year and a monthly publishes only 12, a weekly can gross as much as 433 percent more in advertising revenue than a monthly can. Second, which may be even more important, the more frequently a magazine appears, the more timely its contents can be—increasing competition from broadcast media has created greater emphasis on timeliness. Third, a weekly publication may benefit from a reader's habit. He may establish a pattern of reading a magazine at a certain time each week.

Regional Editions.   Although a magazine may have nationwide or even worldwide circulation, it still is possible to buy specific regional coverage in an increasing number of magazines. Magazines such as *Time, Playboy, Better Homes and Gardens, Sports Illustrated,* and the *Reader's Digest*

---

[1] "Some Observations and Thoughts Relating to Advertising Research," Daniel Starch and Staff, Inc., 1971.

offer the interested advertiser a choice of "regional editions" in which he can place an ad at far less cost than one for the entire circulation would be. These editions are identical in editorial content, but they give local advertisers a chance to buy space in only those copies that will circulate within a specific geographic region.

Regional editions offer the local or regional advertiser the opportunity to enjoy the prestige of national magazine advertising for a limited budget. Most readers do not even realize that an ad is limited to a regional edition, for the only identification is a tiny code number at the bottom of the page.

A growing number of business magazines also offer regional advertising options, a boon to the smaller advertiser who previously has had no mass advertising outlet other than direct mail.

Some publications even allow the advertiser to decide the number of copies within a region in which he wants his ad to appear. The advertiser sometimes can choose groups of ZIP codes, cities, or counties to which he wants his selected quantity of copies to be sent. Some magazines make almost any combination of quantities and localities available to an advertiser, based on a set fee plus a cost per thousand copies. Thus, an advertiser wishing to saturate the magazine's circulation in the Milwaukee area can do so easily, the only limiting factor being a minimum quantity requirement.

Radio

The power, size, and influence of the broadcast media—radio and television—make it difficult to remember that both are relatively young. Commercial radio broadcasting began in 1920, and television as a commercial medium dates from the period immediately following World War II. Color television has been important only since the 1960s.

Despite the traditional popularity of print media and the tremendous growth of television, radio continues to remain an important advertising medium. It is a truly mass medium, for nearly everyone owns a radio and is free to switch the dial on that radio to whatever type of programming he wants to hear. Because radio is "mass" rather than "selective," radio advertising consists almost entirely of advertisements of consumer products and services. Only rarely do industrial or wholesale marketers use radio advertising to try to reach their business customers, and in those rare cases when they do, such advertising is likely to be more the image-building than the sales-generating type.

Station Types. The "standard" broadcast stations are the amplitude modulation (AM) stations; some are local, with a limited range, while more powerful stations extend their signal for considerable distances. An AM station's power may be 250 or 500 watts (local), 1,000 or 5,000 watts (regional), or up to 50,000 watts. Pending legislation may increase the present 50,000-watt AM ceiling. Increasingly popular today are the frequency modulation (FM) stations, all of which have a relatively short range (a 50-mile radius is rare) and usually are limited to a metropolitan area.

AM stations usually have larger audiences not only because their signal extends a greater distance but also because there are more AM receivers than FM receivers. FM has its own advantage: FM signals are not affected by buildings, tunnels, or lightning, and FM can, within its listening area, offer static-free sound.

Prime Times. In today's television-oriented market, the prime commercial radio time is the morning "drive time," from 6 a.m. to 9 a.m., Monday through Friday. The next best time is the evening drive time, from 4 p.m. to 7 p.m., Monday through Friday. This reflects the immense importance of car radios, for the only radio-listening some people do is while driving to and from work. Adding to the importance of these times, however, is the radio-listening done by the family in the morning: weather and correct time can be important for every member of the family, and most stations repeat the forecast and the time frequently throughout the early morning hours.

In addition to prime-time spots, many stations offer special-interest programming. The advertiser can place his commercials in or adjacent to programs of particular interest to a particular group. Sports programs, for instance, have a strong majority of men listeners, whereas the audiences between 10 a.m. and 4 p.m. are mainly female. There also are some stations that concentrate on special kinds of programs or special ethnic groups. An increasing number of stations offer little except news. There are foreign-language stations, stations that beam their programs at the black community, and stations that are teen-oriented.

```
        WPAT-FM Progam Log for Tuesday, November 6, 1973

  2-00:08:47A  0747  NFF  01000  WPAT-FM JINGLE ID
  2-00:09:00A  0100  NFS         WPAT-FM MUSIC
  2-00:09:01A  0100  NFS         WPAT-FM MUSIC
  2-00:25:21A  0400  NFS         WPAT-FM MUSIC (FILL)
  2-00:27:26A  0748  NFF         WPAT-FM JINGLE
  2-00:27:36A  0724  NFF         NEWS
  2-00:28:48A  0525  NFF  00701  WHITES ELECTION DAY SALE     :30CM
  2-00:29:31A  0606  NFF  00737  WALLACHS                 :60  CM
  2-00:30:00A  0507  NFF  00232  EVEREADY BATTERIES           :60CM
  2-00:31:10A  0200  NFS         WPAT-FM MUSIC
  2-00:31:11A  0200  NFS         WPAT-FM MUSIC
  2-00:41:05A  0400  NFS         WPAT-FM MUSIC (FILL)
  2-00:43:48A  0400  NFS         WPAT-FM MUSIC (FILL)
  2-00:46:47A  0748  NFF         WPAT-FM JINGLE
  2-00:46:59A  0735  NFF         WEATHER
  2-00:47:20A  0505  NFF  00038  TWA/AMBASSADOR          :60 CM
  2-00:48:21A  0641  NFF  00154  FRANKLIN NATIONAL BANK  :60CM
  2-00:49:22A  0607  NFF  00563  CARROLLON/PUNT E MES   :60CM
  2-00:50:23A  0300  NFS         WPAT-FM MUSIC
  2-09:03:00A  0300  NFS         WPAT-FM MUSIC
  2-09:05:41A  0400  NFS         WPAT-FM MUSIC (FILL)
  2-09:07:38A  0747  NFF  01000* PAT-FM JINGLE ID
  2-09:07:46A  0735  NFF         WEATHER
  2-09:08:09A  0501  NFF  516   * ALITALIA                 :60 CM
  2-09:09:08A  0516  NFF  00183  RIPLEY CLOTES           :60 CM
  2-09:10:10A  0511  NFF  00055  DATSUN DEALERS    :60 CM
```

Courtesy of WPAT, Clifton, N.J.

This sample page from a computer printout of a radio program log shows a station's morning schedule. Which hours are considered prime time?

The Cumulative Effect. Many advertisers consider radio the least expensive and most effective medium of all for creating and maintaining an image. The retailer whose catchy jingle is heard every day of every week for several years never needs to wonder whether his name and his company's slogan will be remembered. The repetition has that important synergistic effect, gradually snowballing in its memory-retentive effect on listeners. The "Avon Calling!" jingle was the single most important image-builder for that company.

Radio advertising's cumulative effect is aided by the fact that a radio ad dominates the station while that ad is being broadcast. To anyone listening, that ad is all that can be heard. Unlike the situation in the average newspaper or magazine, in radio no other ads can interrupt the attention of the potential customer.

Television

The medium with the most power—and the one with the most question marks for the local advertiser—is television. As an instant trendmaker, no other medium compares with television. Some programs are watched simultaneously by one of every four men, women, and children in the country. A national audience measured in the tens of millions is not extraordinary for the first showing of a popular feature film or for a major sports event. Overnight the product advertised on such a program becomes familiar to the entire country.

Station Types. There are two sets of television channels, or bands: the very-high-frequency (VHF) channels, numbered 2 to 13 on the dial and the ultra-high-frequency (UHF) channels, numbered 14 to 83.

Even though, for some years, all television sets sold in the United States have been required by federal law to include all channels, many UHF stations have had difficulty attracting audiences of a size equivalent to the VHFs in the same market. One reason for this is that, on most receivers, the VHF stations snap into place with individual tuning, whereas the UHF stations must be hand-tuned by a sliding dial. In some ways UHF, which came into being later than VHF, has problems parallel to those which for years made it difficult for FM radio stations to compete.

Prime Times. Early morning through midafternoon programming usually is aimed at women. Later afternoon programming is child-oriented. Evening shows are apt to be "mass" in that they appeal to the entire family, with emphasis on adult entertainment increasing as the hour grows later. Late evening programming is largely aimed at men, and Sunday during the day is a potpourri with religion, intellectual appeal, sports, and mass-appeal programs all appearing, depending on station and season.

Production Costs. With all its power, there is no medium in which a mistake is as costly as television. A single commercial may cost the national advertiser with a sense of flair $75,000 to $150,000. If that commercial is unsuccessful, he has wasted not only his production cost but the cost of the time he has bought to exhibit the commercial.

It might be thought that the laws of economics would declare a $100,000 commercial to be an impossible investment. Yet, that commercial might cost less per viewer reached than the local advertiser's $1,000 commercial: If the $100,000 commercial is aired ten times and has an average audience of 10,000,000 viewers each time it is aired, then with a total audience of 100 million viewers, the cost per exposure is 1/10 cent per viewer.

However, if the $1,000 commercial is aired ten times and has an average audience of 10,000 viewers each time it is aired, then with a total audience of 100,000 viewers, the cost per exposure is 1 cent per viewer—ten times as much as the $100,000 commercial.

This example exposes another problem: Because television audiences have become used to lavish production both in programming and in commercials, many potential local advertisers feel that the limitations of their finances, rather than those of the medium, prevent them from using television effectively.

Types of Commercials. The 60-, 30-, 20-, and 10-second commercials that are scheduled between programs or within a "participating" program are known as "spot broadcasts." They offer the greatest flexibility to the advertiser, since he does not tie his advertising to a single program that, if unpopular or unsuccessful, represents a great dollar waste. Until the late 1960s, television commercials were of three lengths: 60 seconds, 20 seconds, and 10 seconds. The 30-second commercial, which in the mid-1960s was available on only a handful of stations, now has become the most popular length.

An advertiser may also choose full program sponsorship. The sponsor of a complete program enjoys the benefit of total association with that program, the carry-over of loyalty the viewer may feel to that program, and all the commercials within the show, plus a sponsor mention at the beginning and end.

Another option is joint program sponsorship. A baseball game or a regular dramatic program may be sponsored by several companies whose products do not conflict. For example, a beer company, an insurance company, and a gasoline company may each sponsor one-third of the program. The cost to each is reduced, and the station's revenue is greater, since each cosponsor pays perhaps 40 percent of what a single sponsor might have paid.

Although a company cannot place advertisements on public television, it can sponsor programs. Educational television stations regularly broadcast programs whose title states, "Made possible by a grant from XYZ

Corporation." Large companies, by making dollars available for the production of such programs, are building images for themselves.

Barter. "Trading" for broadcast time is a sophisticated arrangement that until the early 1970s was known to only a handful of bulk time buyers. A few years later, broadcast barter had become known and available to thousands of local and national time-buyers.

Originally, barter was just that: someone who had mechandise, from ball-point pens to automobiles or travel, would trade it to a radio or television station for commercial time equivalent to the retail cost of the merchandise. Or, someone who supplied a station with a program would accept full or partial payment in commercial time rather than in dollars.

Ultimately, as some of these barterers controlled more time than they themselves could use, they began to sell it to other broadcast advertisers and a new industry was born. Today, most stations (including many that offer barter time) still dismiss barter as a flea in the ear, but the Federal Communications Commission reported a 1972 barter figure of almost $55 million for television alone, some 4.6 percent of total spot sales and about twice the amount reported for 1971.

One reason for the stations' dismissal of barter as a minuscule by-product of spot buying is that if the majority of advertisers seek out one of the big-volume barter services, station rate cards will be meaningless. The cost of time bought through a barter company averages 10 to 30 percent below normal rates.

However, stations dealing in barter time—and many stations allow no barter time—will not permit spots bought by barter to run if the advertiser has, within the past year, bought time direct from the station or through its sales representative.

Aside from the problem of unavailability of barter time on many stations, another problem faced by the discount buyer is that his spots are preemptible and will not be guaranteed to run should the station be able to sell that same time at the rate-card price. At Christmas time or during election week, when stations may be sold out, the barter buyer can be squeezed out of the marketplace.

But even its detractors agree that barter is a growing, if complicated, business trend.

With videotaping came fewer errors—and increased production costs, making television a more expensive medium than it was in the days of the "live" commercial.

The Local Advertiser. In television's early days, when stations were local in both programming and attitude and networks had yet to grow to their present size, even relatively small local businessmen found television not only exciting but also profitable and low in cost as a type of retail advertising exposure. Many an automobile dealer became the leading dealer in his area by sponsoring telecasts of feature movies and coverage of sports events, with himself as the on-camera announcer for the commercials. Today, television is too expensive a medium for the smaller retailers, except in the tiniest markets or on the least effective stations.

The skyrocketing rise in television advertising costs (a 60-second commercial that cost $50 in the middle 1950s costs from 10 to 20 times that amount today) has been due in part to the increase in production costs—the day of the "live" commercial is over. Gone are the mistakes and forgotten words that used to add to television's entertainment value but cause chagrin to the sponsor.

Almost all present-day commercials are prepared on film or videotape. (Improved efficiency and lowered costs in videotape production have brought some local advertisers back to television.) The addition of color also adds to the cost.

But the increase in the cost of television time is due mostly to the enormous saturation of sets and the vastly increased size of audiences. On a per-viewer basis, television may be a better buy today. Yet the small advertiser simply cannot afford the price; and the marginal advertiser, whose location may not be accessible to the entire metropolitan area served by the TV station or whose product or service may not appeal to the mass audience, may experience substantial wastage; he may be paying to reach people who cannot or will not buy what he has to sell. Other media will have a more realistic coverage for him.

Loss of revenue from a prime source—cigarettes—prompted stations to take a second look at the local advertiser. During 1970, cigarette manufacturers collectively spent $190,000,000 on television advertising.[2] As of 1971, an act of Congress banned such advertising altogether.

Another source of revenue loss came in the fall of 1971, when "network option time"—that period of the evening during which a network affiliate station's programming is controlled by the network—was trimmed by three and one-half hours each week or half an hour a day. (Previously, depending on the time zone, network option time was either 6 to 10 p.m. or 7 to 11 p.m.)

The Federal Communications Commission order that reduced network option time gave back control to the stations of an extra half hour, and that extra local programming has meant extra commercials available to local advertisers who previously were squeezed out of the key time periods.

(Objections and criticisms by stations and networks alike had many broadcast sources predicting that the half hour soon would be restored to the networks.)

What is available to the local advertiser during network option time? Within any market area, the three most important television stations are likely to be network affiliates; other stations in the area operate as independents. Thus the local advertiser has a better opportunity to compete with the national advertisers who sponsor network programs if he

[2] *Advertising Age,* January 11, 1971, page 86.

negotiates with the unaffiliated stations, if any; on the other hand, such stations may have a lower listenership because their programming is local, syndicated, or reruns purchased from the networks that showed the program series previously.

Assuming that time is available, is there any incentive for the local advertiser? The businessman who looks for a local rate card from his television station, similar to the retail rate offered by his local newspaper, is likely to be disappointed. Most television stations have one rate that applies to all buyers. Since that rate is commissionable to advertising agencies, there are many circumstances in which the businessman who handles his own advertising elsewhere may have an advertising agency handle his television campaign.

Direct Mail

Not exactly an advertising medium, yet not exactly a sales promotion technique, direct mail (sometimes called direct advertising) is the most important advertising method for many businessmen; often direct mail is the only advertising method they use.

("Direct advertising," as a trade term, usually means mailed materials, but the field also includes handouts, such as circulars distributed to passersby or door to door.)

No other form of advertising offers such total flexibility of budget. A businessman can start a direct mail campaign with a budget of $100 or with a budget of $1,000,000. He is in complete control of the campaign and does not have to depend on newspaper production men who may put his ad next to his competitor's or on radio announcers who may sound bored while reading his commercial; nor need he concern himself about on which page or at what time his ad appears.

The concern the businessman does have is the competitive nature of the materials in his customers' mailboxes. Veteran large-scale users of direct mail tend to be able to predict the percentage of response a particular direct mail offer will attract. They claim that certain neighborhoods and parts of the country respond better to mail received on a particular day; that different colors generate different types of response; and that the production of a piece of direct mail is as important as the message it contains. But other experts claim that recipients will respond to the message, not the medium, and add that it is possible in direct mail—as in every other medium—to overproduce the message.

A direct mail campaign can be as simple as having a secretary type copies of a standard sales letter in her spare moments; but a typical direct mail campaign involves writing copy, choosing formats, deciding on enclosures, and finding the right mailing lists, each in itself an important job.

Costs have risen sharply in direct mail, and they continue to rise. Today's high cost of any extensive use of direct mail has led the giants in the field to intensify the search for methods and techniques to help improve response. Years ago, a mailing that pulled a 2 percent response was considered successful; today, a 10 percent response may barely pay for the cost of the mailing itself.

In spite of the rising costs, direct advertising still pours into every mailbox, and a surprising number of companies consider direct mail advertising the backbone of their sales promotion.

Specialty Advertising

Advertising specialty salesmen claim, "If it exists, it's a possible advertising medium." Almost every imaginable item has been used for advertising, from people (carrying sandwich signs or even personally painted with advertising slogans) to packets of needles. Advertising appears on fans, caps, ballpoint pens, buttons, decals, key chains, ashtrays, wallets, calendars, notepads, desk sets, books, maps—and thousands of other items. The two leading specialty items are calendars and matchbooks.

The businessman who distributes desk calendars every Christmas is planting on each desk a piece of advertising that will be seen every day of the coming year. This may be one reason for the popularity of calendars as specialty advertising items; calendars account for one-third of all the money spent on specialty advertising.

Almost everyone, smoker or not, is exposed to matchbook advertising. Such advertising usually is nothing more than the name of the business, most commonly a restaurant or hotel, on the outside of the matchbook. Correspondence schools and mail-order insurance companies also make use of matchbook advertising, often using the inside of the matchbook as a coupon.

A single company may have its imprint on millions of matchbooks each year, but the cost is truly nominal considering that each matchbook advertising message may have 20 separate exposures, being seen each time the owner lights a match. Repeated exposure of the same advertising message at no additional cost to the advertiser is impossible in the mass media, and the multiple impact of the matchbook message can be an effective means of persuasion.

Usually the advertiser deals with a matchbook company, which guarantees distribution of a specific number of matchbooks within a specific period of time. These matchbooks are dispensed from cigarette vending machines or are distributed by restaurants, supermarkets, and any other businesses that do not print their own matchbooks. Distribution to the point of sale, however, does not necessarily mean immediate distribution to the public, and even after a matchbook gets into someone's hands it is entirely possible for years to elapse between the use of the first match and the use of the twentieth. It is not unknown for a matchbook coupon offering a correspondence course or a discount auto insurance plan to be mailed a decade after it was printed.

Other Specialty Items. Improvements in communications and the alertness of businessmen have led to the establishment of many additional advertising possibilities. None of these offers the potential for instant mass communication that the print and broadcast media offer, but, because of their novelty value and because of their noncompetitive nature, each has attracted a growing number of users. None can be considered a major advertising medium, and it would be dangerous for a marketer to allocate his total advertising budget to one of them. However, they can be used successfully for a one-shot promotion, and their unusual approach often achieves the desired impact.

A telegram is the one sure way to reach a customer who is unavailable by telephone and who does not answer (and perhaps does not even read) his mail. Because of the combination of urgency and personalization that a telegram conveys, it can be remarkably effective. However, a telegram is probably one of the most expensive means of advertising communication. It also is a one-way communication that cannot, in itself, encourage a reply through a coupon or return envelope.

If a user sends the identical message to a number of people, Western Union will allow a discount below normal telegram rates. Other discount rates are available for night letters, day letters, and communications sent to a single geographic area.

The radio station that sends out transistor radios permanently tuned to that single station is assuring itself of listening loyalty, for there is no way to tune the set to a different station.

Balloons are traditionally popular among advertisers, for every helium-filled balloon carried down the street by a child attracts attention both to the balloon itself and to the name of the company imprinted on it.

Another kind of balloon advertising available in limited markets is the Goodyear blimp, for that company, on occasion, accepts advertising that appears on the blimp as a continuously moving sign with letters several feet tall.

Skywriting is a form of advertising that has shown much technical improvement over the last few years. At one time, the single plane attempting to spell out "Pepsi Cola" might find that the "PE" had blown into meaningless wisps before the "SI" had been completed. Today, however, brief slogans can be written in the sky by several planes working in unison, capable of spelling out the message in a fraction of the time it used to take. Colored smoke is available. And some writings are actually computer-controlled.

Airplane-towed signs are popular in many urban areas. Originally limited to vacation areas such as Miami Beach, the towed sign has appeared over many cities in recent years. Some cities ban their use, fearing that the sign may fall and hurt people below, but the improved strength of the towlines have convinced other areas that they are safe.

These are just a few of the novelty forms of advertising that businessmen might find intriguing and useful.

Outdoor Advertising

Billboards that meet the standards of size, design, and method of construction established by the Outdoor Advertising Association of America are classified as outdoor advertising. Some admen regard nonstandardized signs as a separate medium.

Outdoor advertising helps national advertisers give impetus to an advertising campaign by frequently repeating a slogan used in other media.

Outdoor advertising is useful for delivering messages to drivers about products that are used on the highway, such as oil and tires, or service businesses on or near the highway, such as restaurants or motels. It also helps to remind people about familiar products so that they will remember to buy them when they go shopping. The best outdoor advertising presents a clear, brief, and pointed message, and its bright colors and large illustrations attract the prospective customer's attention.

Transit Advertising

Transit advertising is placed in buses, subways, commuter trains, and bus, airline, and railroad stations. It is aimed at the more than 8 billion people who use these methods of transportation yearly.

Car cards, traveling displays, and station posters are forms of transit advertising. Car cards are the advertising messages found in the interior of buses, subway and commuter trains, and taxis. Traveling displays are advertising messages placed on the outside of buses. Station posters are located in subways, railroad stations, bus terminals, and airline terminals and are often used in conjunction with a car card campaign.

Transit advertising is important to advertisers who want to remind customers of products that they can buy when they leave the vehicle. Since many customers are exposed to the advertisement, its cost per viewer is relatively low. Also, such advertising has the reader's attention for a comparatively long period and thus can make a lasting impression. Both national and local advertisers use transit advertising. One of the largest national advertisers to use transit advertising is Wrigley's Chewing Gum; cigarette manufacturers also are frequent transit advertisers. Local retail and service firms find this type of advertising valuable in reaching commuters and shoppers.

Media Rates

Each publication, broadcast station, outdoor sign company, or other public advertising medium publishes a rate card. This card lists advertising rates, circulation information, issuance and closing dates, and mechanical requirements such as page size and column width in the case of newspapers and magazines, or type of slide and film accepted in the case of television stations.

Even within a limited field of interest, compiling a complete list of rate cards is a difficult task. In a rapidly changing economy, furthermore, rates change.

Standard Rate and Data Service publishes on a monthly or quarterly basis large paperbound volumes that quote current rates for various media. Typical volumes published on a monthly basis are those listing rates for newspapers, consumer magazines and farm publications, business publications, radio broadcast stations, and television broadcast stations.

Generally, rates published in Standard Rate and Data publications are "national" rates—that is, the rate listed includes a commission for an advertising agency and for a sales representative from the publication. Many newspapers give retailers a lower rate, called a "local" or "retail" rate.

At one time the advertiser seeking orders direct from readers, viewers, or listeners could pay some media on a per-inquiry basis; but per inquiry or "p. i. deals" went into eclipse in the mid-1950s and have not re-emerged. Most media no longer accept them.

SALES PROMOTION METHODS

The businessman who assumes that his advertising represents, in itself, the maximum weight his promotion dollars can bring is missing many important sales promotion opportunities: Advertising is just a part of the total effort—often by far the largest part, in terms of budgeted dollars, it is true, but still only a part. A total campaign, to be effective, uses all the promotion tools.

One sales promotion tool is publicity, which might be described as a kind of free advertising; displays, both window and interior, are very important to retail stores; exhibits, set up at trade shows and conventions, are a means of sales promotion important to industrial and wholesale marketers. Still other tools of sales promotion range from the ordinary telephone to the extraordinary audiovisual devices being developed.

These sales promotion methods and tools not only have their individual impact in generating sales and creating and maintaining image, but they also add to the synergistic effect of the total campaign. If the theme that highlights the advertising is promoted through publicity, repeated in displays, and underlined in exhibits, it is unlikely that prospective customers will not have been exposed to that theme and, it is hoped, influenced by it.

Magazine Antiques, The

Media Code 8 052 0867 5.00
Published monthly by Straight Enterprises, Inc., 551 Fifth Ave., New York, N. Y. 10017. Phone 212-682-8282.

PUBLISHER'S EDITORIAL PROFILE
MAGAZINE ANTIQUES, THE is edited for collectors of antiques and works of art, and for students of early American social history and culture. Feature articles deal with furniture, painting, sculpture, prints, architecture, ceramics, glass, textiles, metals, living with antiques in your home, the art and history of collecting, and American subjects, the arts and antiquities of western European countries and England are covered over the seventeenth through the nineteenth centuries. Regular monthly columns include news of current exhibitions, recent acquisitions of museums, notes on collectors and collecting, the English antiques field, and book reviews. Rec'd 5/22/73.

1. PERSONNEL
Publisher—Arthur S. Gibbons.
Editor—Wendell Garrett.
Business Manager—William Hillpot.
2. REPRESENTATIVES and/or BRANCH OFFICES
Los Angeles—Grace Norman-Wilcox.
London—Tony Keniston.
Amsterdam—F. D. Beuther.
France—Denise Dryfuss.
Germany—Okka C. Fuehrer.
3. COMMISSION AND CASH DISCOUNT
15% to agencies on display rates if paid within 30 days. Cash discount 2% on current invoices paid by 10th of month of issue. No discount on classified and directory units.
4. GENERAL RATE POLICY

ADVERTISING RATES
Rates effective January 1, 1973.
Rates received August 25, 1972.

5. BLACK/WHITE RATES

	1 ti	3 ti	6 ti	12 ti
1 page	1217.	1104.	986.	867.
1/2 page	615.	556.	499.	438.
1/4 page	316.	289.	259.	237.
1/8 page	170.	156.	139.	122.

Special rates: 1 page or more in 12 consecutive issues, 797.00 per page. 10% discount (from applicable rates above) on 2 or more full page insertions in any issue (must be full page facing units).

"The Attic":	1 ti	3 ti	6 ti	12 ti
Single unit (1/32 pg.)	52.	-----	40.	35.

Maximum size of 1 insertion is 2 units (vertical only). Double unit counts only as 1 insertion on 6 or 12 time contract. No illustrative material accepted.
Real Estate:
The Attic and general advertising rates apply. No illustrative material accepted for less than a 1/8 page ad. Horizontal double unit permitted.
6. COLOR RATES

4 color:	1 ti	3 ti	6 ti	12 ti
1 page	500.	400.	300.	200.
1/2 page	375.	300.	250.	150.

To earn 3, 6, or 12 time rate for color, advertiser must take the required number of color insertions regardless of the number of black and white insertions he takes.

8. INSERTS
Rates and requirements available.
9. BLEED
1/2 pages, extra _____ 5%
No charge for full pages.
10. SPECIAL POSITION
Extra (other than covers) _____ 10%
11. CLASSIFIED AND READING NOTICES
CALENDAR OF SHOWS
18.00 per maximum 2 line listing. Limit of 2 listings per show.
CLEARING HOUSE
.75 per word. 18.00 minimum charge per insertion. Name and address or box number c/o Antiques count as 2 words. Antique dealers are not permitted to advertise items for sale.
HISTORIC HOUSES
75.00 per year. 40.00 for 6 months for basic listing of 6 lines. Additional billed at 25.00 per line (flat rate, 6 or 12 months).
HOUSE & GARDEN TOURS
20.00 per minimum 2 line listing; 6.00 per additional line.
TRAVEL GUIDE
Published quarterly. Maximum 3 line listing. Orders only on calendar year or remainder of calendar year.

Closing date:	Issues	Charge
Jan. 1	March, June, Sept., Dec.	37.
Apr. 1	June, Sept., Dec.	31.
July 1	Sept., Dec.	25.

14. CONTRACT AND COPY REGULATIONS
See Contents page for location—items 2, 9, 12, 13, 24, 32, 35, 36, 41.
15. MECH. REQUIREMENTS (Web Fed offset)
For complete, detailed production information, see SRDS Print Media Production Data.
Trim size: 9-1/4 x 12.
Binding method: Side wire.
Insert colors available: AAAA/ABP; 4-Color Process (AAAA/MPA).

DIMENSIONS—AD PAGE

1	7-13/16 x 10-1/2	1/4	3-13/16 x 5-1/8
1/2	7-13/16 x 5-1/8	1/8	3-13/16 x 2-1/2
1/2	3-13/16 x 10-1/2		

16. ISSUE AND CLOSING DATES
Published monthly; on sale 1st of publication month. Insertion orders must reach publisher 1st of 2nd month preceding date of issue. Original copy and photos close 7th of 2nd month preceding. Conversion materials close 21st of 2nd preceding month. Offset film closes last day of 2nd month preceding date of issue.
Insertion orders for 4 color ads must reach publisher by 1st of 3rd month preceding publication; color separations or transparency due 1st of 2nd month preceding publication.
No cancellations accepted after closing date.
18. CIRCULATION
Established 1922. Single copy 2.00; per year 16.00. Summary data—for detail see Publisher's Statement.
CPM—B/W 16.69.
A.B.C. 6-30-73 (6 mos. aver.—Magazine Form)

Tot. Pd. (Subs.)	(Single)	(Assoc.)
72,170	71,882	288	....

Average Total Non-Pd Distribution (not incl. above): Total 750
TERRITORIAL DISTRIBUTION 4/73—72,737

N.Eng.	Mid.Atl.	E.N.Cen.	W.N.Cen.	S.Atl.	E.S.Cen.
10,082	18,477	9,633	2,728	16,342	4,280
W.S.Cen.	Mtn.St.	Pac.St.	Canada	Foreign	Other
4,022	1,077	4,760	688	450	198

(C-C.C-B)

This listing from Standard Rate and Data Service gives the rates for advertising in one consumer magazine.

Publicity

Some businessmen do not understand publicity and assume that it represents another promotional cost that they are unwilling or unable to bear. Others know and understand its use but feel that they will appear demanding if they ask for press coverage. Neither position is valid; *publicity* is the nonpaid mention of a business by the media because something the business is doing is of interest to the public.

Usually, there is at least one facet of any product or service that is newsworthy: There is a new automobile insurance rate or the fall fashions are in or prices have been cut on a wide range of lamps or a new line of plumbing fixtures is being introduced or an unusual foreign car is on the lot. Any one of these items is a legitimate theme for publicity. It is the editors of the media who will decide what material to use and how much of it to use; therefore, publicity is not used unless it contains elements that are truly newsworthy or information in which the publication's readers or the broadcast audience will be interested.

Publicity does have a cost attached to it: as with advertising, publicity material should be prepared in a professional manner, in terms of copy and of artwork or photographs that will appeal to an editor. When this material is used, however, it appears as news, not as advertising, and since news is usually considered to be unbiased, the publicity item has strong impact on the potential customers.

Display

For the retailer, displays are the single most important sales promotion tool. Only advertising may be more powerful in improving sales. Advertising may interest customers in a product, but window displays stop passersby in the street and bring them into the store, and interior displays attract and direct those customers and identify the merchandise for them. Displays usually are worked out to coordinate with advertising, so that what is being advertised also is featured in displays; but displays also create impulse sales, sales made to customers who have not seen any advertising of the products.

In addition to generating sales, displays are an important factor in creating and maintaining image. An exclusive jewelry store may have half a dozen rings or a few bracelets placed on a square of velvet as the sole display in a small window. A variety store, on the other hand, may pack its windows with tiers of merchandise, each item displaying a large price tag. Both stores not only are displaying their products but also are underscoring the image they want to project.

Professional display specialists usually handle the more elaborate displays in the bigger stores, but, often, the smaller departmental displays are worked out by those working in the department—and in the specialty shops, the owner often does his window work himself.

A poor display is simply dead space, but the advantages of a good display are immediately obvious because of the people who stop to look and then perhaps to buy.

Perhaps some of the most spectacular displays, however, are designed to create goodwill rather than to build sales. During the Christmas season, the major department stores in most cities vie with each other in designing elaborate and extravagant Christmas window displays. Their appeal is so strong that people often have to line up for a chance to look at the windows. Most of these windows emphasize a theme rather than a collection of merchandise—and yet the mood they project obviously results in sales, too.

Exhibits

Marketers in the industrial and wholesale fields often use trade show and convention exhibits to give their wares optimum exposure. Space can be expensive, and exhibits can be troublesome to design, set up, and man; yet the people who attend these business shows usually are ideal prospective customers, for it is their involvement with a particular trade or profession or business that brings them to the convention or trade show.

Even for the smallest company, showmanship is demanded of a convention or trade show exhibit. Leaving its design and construction to amateurs or to executives who are not promotion-oriented can result in a dull and stodgy image for the company. Those prospective customers attending the meeting have only the exhibit, and the people manning it, as their image of the parent company.

Some exhibits are expected to produce actual sales. Others are designed to give exposure to a product or a company and to collect names of prospective customers who can be contacted at some future date. In either case, the exhibit is almost always manned by professional salesmen.

An exhibit can be as simple as a rack display of a company's products, or it can be as elaborate as a miniature theater where prospective customers watch a color movie about the company and its products before moving on to a lounge to discuss with a company representative any questions they may have.

Audiovisual Tools

Many exhibits, as well as many salesmen making their sales presentations, now use new, compact audiovisual tools to capture and keep the attention of prospective customers. These include slides, filmstrips, motion pictures, videotape, and tape and disc recordings. In an office presentation, slides can be projected on a miniature screen that sits on the customer's desk, and motion pictures can be shown through the equivalent of a television screen.

A slide projector is perhaps the least expensive of the audiovisual tools, for slides are easier to prepare than films. With a simple slide projector, a real estate salesman can show his customer a succession of pictures of the houses and apartments he has available, an industrial salesman can show a client not only his entire product line but also glimpses of the techniques that were used to produce it, or an insurance broker can underline the benefits of the policy he is trying to sell by using slides that turn the benefits into pictures.

Videocassettes and EVR, "electronic video recording," are the newest and most elaborate of the tools available. They enable film or videotape to be played through ordinary television receivers, thus eliminating the need for special projection equipment.

These tools, which put action into an advertising and sales promotion campaign, are in a state of change because of constant technological improvements. Motion picture techniques, unchanged for years, suddenly are growing, expanding, changing, and occasionally simplifying.

Electronic sales aids are being invented at a rate that confounds the patent office. The businessman who wants to be competitive must stay abreast of these changes and should study the trade publications, attend shows and conventions, and investigate the new techniques. The dazzling new developments enable all businessmen to do a better job of selling.

NOW, APPLY WHAT YOU'VE LEARNED

Test your ability to choose among the advertising and sales promotion media, based on the information in this chapter.

1. Obtain rate cards from local newspapers and broadcast stations. Analyze the comparative rates based on audience reached.

2. Using the rate cards obtained above, plan a 90-day promotion for the opening of a new car dealership. The budget is $5,000; justify the media used.

3. You operate a small distributorship of display fixtures that you sell to retail stores. Your annual advertising and promotion expenditure has been $2,500. You now decide to build greater volume and project an image for your business. What would you do? What would you spend?

4. Using one medium only, build the image of a department store as, "The Store With More—for Less!" The store has an annual budget of $50,000 for all advertising and promotion. Decide how much of this you will use to build this particular image and over what period of time.

5. You manufacture farm equipment that attaches to a tractor and in one unit tills, plants, and fertilizes corn. You must prepare materials for your local dealers to use for advertising and local promotion. Since you have no budget for this, you allocate $3,000. How would you spend it?

6. You are a salesman for a local radio station. A furniture store owner tells you he does not believe that radio pulls customers for his type of business. Prepare a campaign for him which outlines the use of your station. Specify times when his broadcasts would be on the air and why.

7. Choose one of these products to manufacture: (a) a professional dry-cleaning machine; (b) a water purifier for soft drink vending machines; (c) a floor-cleaning compound for

use in industrial plants. Assuming that you have 5 percent of the total market, and assuming that last year your total volume was $250,000 with a net profit of $20,000, plan to increase your share of market. What will you do? What will it cost? How will the program be implemented? Write out a complete promotion plan and justify your expenses with an argument in favor of the objectives such expenses will achieve.

8. Plan a campaign to increase the sale of a soft drink within a specific ethnic market.

9. Justify a $1,000 expenditure on a VHF television station in your market to increase the sale of the soft drink; then justify a similar expenditure on a UHF station.

10. As a small distributor of golf carts, your only promotion is an exhibit at a regional trade show attended by about 500 managers of country clubs and golf courses. The space at the show is already paid for; an extra $1,000 is available for materials to be used at the show. How would you spend it?

CHAPTER TWO

Words That Sell

Words are the heart of advertising and sales promotion efforts: words spelling out the theme of a campaign, words in a magazine ad or a radio commercial, words on a display sign. Advertising and sales promotion efforts often succeed simply because of someone's ability to pick effective words and to put them together effectively.

One reason for the care needed in choosing words is that people tend to have lazy memories. In a typical test of memory recall, people were asked to read eight advertisements, and a few minutes later, to give the names of the eight advertisers. The average recall of the group, even after such a short time, was only 5.3 of the eight names.

A second reason is that people have developed a built-in "resistance" to advertising. Their senses are so assaulted by advertising messages from all sides that it takes skill to catch and hold their attention.

For these reasons, words used in advertising and sales promotion need not necessarily be subtle or graceful or elegant or poetic—but they do have to be persuasive: they have to persuade the customer to pay attention; they have to persuade him that their message makes sense; they have to persuade him to buy. To be effective, they must be words that sell.

An old story in the advertising business illustrates that point. One man says to another, "Did you see that horrible-looking Walberg Drugstore ad in today's paper? They had copy about shaving cream for 39 cents smashed up against an item about ice cream for 40 cents a pint, and they had a big black cut for Kaywoodie pipes right next to some delicate linework about Elizabeth Arden cosmetics. And what made the ad look twice as bad was that it was right next to a beautiful full-pager with a gorgeous layout—I forget whose ad that was. . ."

Remember that advertising and sales promotion have two goals: to generate sales and to create and maintain image. In a way, the second goal is really an extension of the first, for image is important only because it helps a company to make sales. If the layout of an ad or the arrangement of a display is so handsome or artistic that it is admired by the customer, that is an added benefit. However, the basic goal of the ad and of the display is to sell, not to win admiration.

This often is less a problem with print ads than it is with radio or television commercials. Some television commercials, for instance (and often they are expensively produced ones) spend so much time trying to be entertaining that they fail in their basic job of trying to sell. In the same way, words, too, can be misused. Copy can be too trite or too clever. It can be oversimplified or overcomplicated. It can be stale or hackneyed or coy.

Obviously, writing brilliant copy requires special talent and practice, but the techniques of writing good, effective, persuasive copy can be learned by almost anyone.

PUTTING PSYCHOLOGY TO WORK

There are a few simple general rules to keep in mind when choosing words to use in persuasion. Adherence to these rules helps produce competent, effective writing—writing that sells.

First, be personal: Remember that when emotion and intellect conflict, emotion always wins. In the world of advertising, this means that the emotional approach, the personal approach, is usually more effective than the intellectual approach, the impersonal approach. "For a more beautiful you" is a line likely to win a cosmetics manufacturer more attention in a women's magazine than, "From the world's most modern laboratories." "Feel the power of a thousand horses" is a stronger appeal for an automobile manufacturer advertising in a sports magazine than, "A cast-aluminum block plus an 11-to-1 compression ratio equals power."

Second, appeal to the ego. Every person is the center of his own world. Appeal to his status consciousness; the impact of that appeal is strong. The same status psychology that makes a young executive feel uneasy driving a five-year-old car (while the older, more secure man may not care at all) or causes a fashion-conscious woman to remove a bargain store label from a dress or brings tears to the eyes of the child who is the only one on the block who doesn't yet have a two-wheeler works in an ad. "They'll think

When an advertiser assumes that his readers know in-group terminology, he alienates those who do not.

you paid $200 for this suit" catches more readers than, "Suits to fit every budget."

Third, use the reader's language. Every marketer should know his target customers. He should know where they live, what they do for a living, how much money they spend and what they like to spend it for, what their interests are, and what their tastes are. These statistical facts about a group of people are called "demographics," and every newspaper and magazine, every radio and television station, can give advertisers demographic information about the audience offered by their medium. Appealing to that audience—in words that are suited to the editorial material—is generally a sound approach to copy: "The day my insurance man stole home" is a more natural line for an insurance company to use in a sports magazine than, "Protection that never ends."

Match the Mood
of the Audience

In analyzing the target audience of advertising, mood is as important as background. For example, does the reader of a car card, inside a bus or subway car, have the time to study an ad? Indeed he does: he may well sit or stand in the same spot for half an hour or more. Yet, his mood is not relaxed, but hurried, because during rush hour the average rider is far from relaxed.

Obviously, no one can predict the state of mind of the reader or viewer at the moment he is exposed to a particular piece of advertising. But generalized yardsticks are available.

The time of day, the month of the year, the geographic location, the national economy, and an individual's own economic circumstances all contribute to his mood and receptivity as he is exposed to advertising.

The Time of Day. The morning mood is one of haste. Time is a specific: if Mr. Brown is not out of his home by 7:50 a.m., he will be late for work; if his son does not leave by 8:10, he will be late for school. A deadline dictates the mood and the amount of time that can be allocated to the listening to and reading of advertising.

In most cities, morning newspapers outcirculate evening papers and carry more advertising as well; morning "drive time" is the most expensive and most sought-after radio time. If people are in such a hurry and are preoccupied to boot, why should this be so?

The answer lies in the raw numbers exposed to the advertising—the cost per thousand. Preoccupied or not, more people listen to the radio in the morning than during any other time of the day (with the possible exception of teen-age-oriented stations, which attract huge 7 p.m. to 11 p.m. audiences among their particular listener groups).

It is true that advertising during the 6 a.m. to 9 a.m. period does not command complete attention; however, it is the one period of the day in which people aggressively seek news and information. So, in theory, advertising aimed at this early morning audience should be straightforward, explicit, and easy to understand.

It is no coincidence that radio and television broadcasts heard weekdays from 6 to 9 a.m. emphasize the time and the weather and condense the news. There is, of course, an afternoon rush hour as well; but during the hours at which workers are driving home, or their families are waiting for them to arrive, the exact time to the minute is not as important; nor is the weather, since the decision to wear a raincoat or galoshes is made in the morning.

Most advertisers know that advertising a "Tuesday Special" in Tuesday's afternoon newspaper is something of a waste, since many readers will not even see the paper until the end of the business day. But they know, too, that there are benefits to reaching people at both times of the day and that urgency is only one of the factors of successful advertising.

Evening is relatively deadline-free. If the Browns are 15 minutes late for their bridge game with a neighbor couple, no problems will result. You might think that this would mean a more intensive readership of the day's evening newspaper. However, the competitive element is stronger in the evening. Radio, television, newspapers, magazines, direct mail, and the trade magazines carried home from the office all compete for attention.

The Day of the Week. Most newspapers publishing both daily and Sunday editions will show, statistically, that more time is spent reading the paper on Sunday. Does this mean that an ad in the Sunday newspaper has a better chance to be read? Not necessarily.

Suppose that a man spends 20 minutes reading his morning newspaper. When Sunday comes, he spends an hour reading the paper. This would mean that an advertiser might expect greater attention on weekends—assuming that the newspaper has the same number of pages. But the Sunday newspaper may be five times thicker than the daily paper, which would mean that each ad receives less attention, not more.

The benefit of weekend reading is that of mood rather than of amount of available time. The reader may be looking for advertising; the week's shopping plans for clothing, appliances, even gifts will be made in concert with the entire family, which often is not assembled together except on weekends.

Mood, then, is considered by many advertising experts to be a key determinant of the power of advertising within a medium. On the other hand, other advertising experts feel that it is possible to overreact to mood; they prefer to generate the mood rather than to become part of it. And it isn't always possible to anticipate mood. The individual who writes the ad may have no idea of the time at which it will appear: placement of the ad is decided in a different department.

KNOWING WHAT YOU ARE SELLING

Often in these pages you may read that "puff" is no substitute for facts. Perhaps the greatest cause of failure in professional advertising copy is the writer's refusal, inability, or lack of interest to learn more about the subject he is trying to sell.

Much advertising copy is the result of pure speculation. This is the copy that is peppered with words such as "beautiful," "unique," "unequalled," and other nondescriptive words, which the writer, lacking specific knowledge, regards as safe. Safe they are; but do they sell? Any good salesman, whether on the floor of a department store, in a product buyer's office, or in public advertising media, will know his product inside out. Advertising a resort without having visited it is sure to result in cliché-ridden copy; advertising a complex industrial machine without understanding its function is sure to result in an oversimplified regurgitation of basic material spoon-fed the writer by the product sales manager; advertising insurance without knowing the particular benefits of the policy being advertised is sure to result in a weak imitation of other copy.

Where to Find Facts

The logical place to find facts about a product is the product itself. Suppose that you are asked to write selling copy for a new electronic instrument. No amount of description can give the information to you that you can glean through an intensive study of the product itself.

Or, suppose that you are asked to handle sales promotion for the Turkish Trade Bureau. A visit to the country will result in a "product knowledge" that far transcends any other source of information.

Or, suppose that you are charged with promotional responsibility for a line of spray paints. Using the paints together with principal competing products is superior to making an armchair assumption that your product is better.

So you must know the "why?" The creative advertising or promotion man who must admit that he is making an assumption without first-hand knowledge does not really know the why; he has homework to do before he can communicate product or service benefit effectively. The automobile salesman who never has driven the car he is trying to sell has an uncertain sales talk coming up.

Facts on Hand. Many products have more information on their labels, their tags, or their instruction manuals than the copywriter could possibly use. This is especially true of appliances, automotive products, furniture, food, musical instruments, recreational and educational materials, and technical products.

The problem is more difficult in the case of services, which are intangible and have no labels. But, unless the service is an entirely new one, there is related material available for study. Lacking this, a valuable approach is to listen to the sales talk of the company's best salesman.

Conversations. Conversations with those charged with the responsibility for sales undoubtedly will result in a notepad filled with useful background information. Obvious as this is, it is a method often bypassed because the individual creating the advertising and sales promotion pieces regards it as a weakness to ask for facts.

The attitude is all the more paradoxical because weakness stems from lack of information, not from pursuit of it.

Conversations with dealers, with users, with experts in the field all will provide useful and often surprising facts about the product or the service. As will be shown later in this chapter, conversations with users often result in powerful advertising copy that can be tied directly to the user's wants and needs.

The Background. The public library is not the only source of background information in every field, but it is the most logical and usually the most accessible. The amount of information available, even in exotic technical fields, is so great that no advertising or sales promotion writer could hope to use it all.

Pamphlets and printed circulars also are available in most fields. Even though they may not relate directly to the specific product being promoted, the background they impart gives expertise and authority to the words being written or spoken.

Trade publications represent the most valuable source of background information. Since they are written to influence those whose state of mind represents the aim of your own promotion, they give penetrating insight into the field. If you advertise a consumer product or service, the technical or trade journals serving the commercial or industrial side of the field being advertised will offer ideas that can be invaluable aids to the advertising or sales promotion writer.

How to Select Pertinent Facts

It is possible for an ad to be so glutted with facts that it fails to communicate. The good copywriter takes one word from the wealth of material available to him: he is "selective." He chooses USEFUL facts from all the information available and achieves strong, selling copy. While puff is no substitute for facts, dull facts are no substitute for useful, interesting ones. If you do nothing more than describe a machine's function, you have overlooked the important reason for promoting a product at all: the why. Why is ours better? Why should the prospect listen? Why are we proud of our product or service? Why, after all, should the buying prospect want to do business with us? These are the facts that result in business.

Before putting any words on paper, any advertising or sales promotion writer, regardless of whether he is a professional or a merchandiser trying to work out his own ideas, should ask himself: "What does the customer want to know? What does the reader want to know? If I were buying, rather than selling, what facts, what arguments would convince me?"

In any sales organization, some salesmen consistently outsell the others. Often this is because these salesmen are able to translate product facts into customer benefits; they are able to look at the product from the customer's point of view. This is exactly what a good writer of advertising and sales promotion copy must do; he must take product information and shape it into strong, solid copy that will attract the customer's interest and sell the product to the customer.

GETTING ATTENTION: THE HEADLINE

The first step in any sales presentation is to capture the customer's attention. In advertising and sales promotion writing, getting attention is the job of the headline, or the opening line, or whatever words are intended to be read or heard first.

(Although most of this chapter's discussion will be in terms of print advertising, the same general rules apply to all written material used in advertising and sales promotion. A radio commercial, for instance, may consist of an opening phrase, effect, or music and a text that parallels the ad's headline and body copy. A display sign often is simply a headline standing by itself.)

It doesn't take a creative genius to write a good headline that demands attention. There are techniques that anyone can use—and it is unfortunate that some professionals ignore these basic tools and depend instead on gimmicks and unbelievable promises and dubious claims. An ad need not have a four-color photo of a nude in order to command attention. Any of these elements can bring attention:

- Size
- Surprise

- Novelty
- Curiosity value

Attention Versus Explanation

Brilliant copy without an attention-getting headline often remains unread. For this reason, the first rule of headline writing is: The headline must command attention, even if its meaning is not immediately or apparently germane to the subject of the ad.

Admittedly, this rule is a simplification, but it does offer safety for the beginner. Obviously, it doesn't mean that a headline should mislead the reader; it does mean that if the choice is between "attention" and "explanation" in the headline, the attention-getting headline will inevitably increase the readership of the written material.

The physical size of the type used for the headline may do the trick—but size is not the only way to get attention. Other attention-getters are words that generate a reaction of surprise, novelty, and curiosity. The average marketer often is working with a smaller ad than the giants in his field; therefore the latter elements can be more important to him. Suppose you saw this headline over a tiny ad:

$26,450 REWARD!

Would you read the ad? Obviously. And the ad might go on to say that the Smith Company (a) saved $26,450 off list prices for customers of its television department or (b) saved $26,450 in insurance premiums for an industrial customer that adopted its new system or (c) saved $26,450 in maintenance costs for a department store chain that installed its new maintenance service, or any of a thousand other possibilities.

To understand this concept, you should understand that the headline attracts readership not because it misleads but because it intrigues. It would have been easier, because it would have required less thought, to head the ad, "Giant television sale" or "Save thousands on insurance" or "Is your maintenance service obsolete?" Any of these headlines would have been workmanlike and accurate, but none of them would have generated as high a readership.

Using "Public Notice" at the top of an ad is neither new nor clever, but one carpet retailer has used it effectively for years. Why? Because these two words overcome the greatest threat to advertising readership: apathy. The reason is obvious: the ad sounds like inside news, something slightly private, information to which the reader normally would not have access.

William Bernbach, Chairman of the Board of the ad agency Doyle Dane Bernbach, once offered these suggestions for writing a good headline: "Catch the eye . . . challenge the mind . . . flatter the wit."[1]

The Danger of Being Clever

Usually, a headline based on a pun is regarded as a trick—but it does get attention, particularly if the pun is either very good or very bad. An ad for diamond rings was headed, "When you decide to altar your plans." An importer for Scotch whiskey referred to his product as "The holiday

[1] David Ogilvy, *Confessions of an Advertising Man*, hard-cover edition, Atheneum Publishing Co., New York, 1963; paperback edition, Dell Publishing Co., New York, 1964.

spirit." A distiller used "Sock it to him," showing a gift decanter in the top of a Christmas sock. A medicated cream was advertised with the line, "Inferiority complexion?" A cruise line had an ad, "Announcing our January white sail."

All catch the attention—but has any of them the simple power of this headline?

> *We put 100 nails in the Sears self-sealing tire.*
> *And then drove it 100 miles.*
> *And it didn't lose a breath of air.*
> *Try that with the tires you're driving around on.*

David Ogilvy, one of the masters of headline writing, has pointed out that a good advertisement sells the product without drawing attention to itself. Too much advertising, especially that written by inexperienced writers who seem to feel that their egos are on the line with their copy, attempts to get the reader to think, "What a clever headline." A headline should call attention to the product. Forced cleverness is assuredly less effective than clear, logical facts about the item being offered.

The theme of an ad is more important than cleverness in phrasing. What is a key fact that will attract the reader's attention? Find that, and it is the key to a good headline. A clothing store ran a headline saying, "We'd stand on our heads to please you," with an illustration of a man standing on his head, holding a suit. The creator of the ad undoubtedly thought he had been clever, but the impact of the ad on the reader was nil. The store tried again, and this time got the business they wanted with an ad that began, "Starting at 9:30 a.m. tomorrow, you can own a $125 suit for $80."

Facts Versus "Puff"

No amount of "puff," or excess verbiage, is a substitute for facts. "The wonderful, wonderful tire that others can only envy" is a poor headline compared with "Three days only: special sale of 4-ply nylon cord tires." From a merchandising point of view, the first headline says nothing; the second gives selling facts. One way of testing a headline for such a deficiency is to see whether it would sound intelligent, interesting, and stimulating as the opening few words in a spoken sales presentation.

Puff also can be the result of trying to sound too folksy, too slangy. Readers like to be spoken to in words they can understand, but they are very sensitive about the slightest hint of a patronizing tone in writing. "Professional Wrestling Tonight" will bring more business than "Watch 'em grunt and groan." "Our coach seats are as wide as first class seats in other airlines" makes more sense than "When you've got it, flaunt it!"

Choosing a Length

Thirty years ago, a headline was supposed to be a single line of type. Today, many successful campaigns are built around headlines that require two, three, or even four lines of type. Advertising writers have learned that readers will take the trouble to read several lines of type, provided that the thought progresses smoothly.

Here are a few examples:

Hong Kong flu or virus cold?
Dristan tablets can relieve more symptoms than
the leading seltzer, aspirin, or any time capsule!

Can Mrs. Reszel's
new Maytag dishwasher
equal the record
of her other Maytags?

These bankers didn't invent the
indestructible golf ball
but they helped get it rolling.

HEART OF THE SELL:
THE BODY COPY

Body copy consists of all written material in an ad other than the headline. Some writers concentrate their imaginations and talents on the headline and pay little attention to the body copy, on the assumption that the headline alone can make the sale.

The headline is intended to attract attention; the body copy is what does the sales job. That the body type is smaller in size than the headline does not diminish its importance. Almost every ad has far more words of body copy than it does of headline copy, and those words, almost as much as the headline, determine whether or not the ad is effective.

Once and for all, American Motors wants you to judge which one of these companies has the best new car guarantee.

A long headline can attract the reader's attention as effectively as a short one. And pertinent, factual body copy will be read.

The Matter of Style

One advertising man will say, "The average reader of an ad has the mentality of a twelve year old." Another advertising man will say, "Never underestimate the intelligence of the reader." Both assumptions are wrong, and both can lead a copywriter into trouble. The middle road is usually the most effective.

The writer whose style shows that he believes the reader to have a childish mentality, having to be led by the hand, usually will lose his readers after the first few lines. Readers will be equally unimpressed by the writer who uses esoteric words and an occasional literary reference to make his point.

The Right Approach. Advertising should be contemporary. It should appeal, in language and in approach, to the target group of customers at whom it is aimed. It should neither talk down to nor over the heads of its target audience.

For instance, terms and words such as "EDP," "Fortran," "Cobol," and "Learn BTAM with 2260s" make sense to those who are computer-oriented, but they may not make sense to those whom an advertiser may be trying to enroll as trainees at a computer school. A doctor knows what "hematoma" is, but the man with a sore leg knows only that he needs something to soothe the pain of a swollen bruise. The mechanic knows what and where the "PCV valve" is, but the average car owner is puzzled unless someone explains positive crankcase ventilation to him.

A surprising approach to copy suggests, "Pretend that you are explaining it to your mother." In other words, don't be patronizing and don't be pompously verbose.

The Problem With Modifiers. Not many advertising men succeed as novelists, because the style they develop tends to be sparse and taut. On the other hand, not many novelists write good advertising copy, because their prose tends to be heavy with adjectives and adverbs, those modifiers that give color and definition to their themes.

"As your fabled iron stallion effortlessly carries you across gently wooded vales, you look forward to the quiet eve when, the gentle hush punctuated only by the soft cat's foot tread of the wheels on the glistening steel bands, you relax on your wondrous Arabian Carpet"—this kind of copy is hardly likely to sell the advantages of a railroad trip. In fact, it is doubtful whether many readers would even know what was being advertised. It has no punch or clarity, because its nouns are vague and there is an overabundance of modifiers to increase that vagueness.

Here is another way of handling the same theme: "So smooth that it is hard to imagine that you are in motion—until you look out the window of your spotless compartment and see the countryside whirl by. If comfort is your pleasure, there really is no other way to travel." Notice how communication with the reader has increased because of the economy in the use of words.

Bullet Copy. In body copy, even more than in headline copy, the writer is tempted to lapse into puff copy, filling out space with useless words. Usually this happens because the facts to be covered are insufficient, in the writer's mind, to fill the space allotted to the body copy.

Rather than try to fill up space by using unnecessary words, it is much better to get more facts—or else to use a bulleted style. *Bullets* are dots placed for emphasis before each item in a list of items or phrases. Asterisks, checkmarks, or other punctuation devices also may be used. Through the use of bullets or other devices, the main selling points of a product often can be given special emphasis. An example of body copy in an ad for an electric iron:

- *Four steam settings, three dry settings*

- *Handles all synthetics easily*

- *Permanent no-stick ironing surface*

- *Lightweight, yet sturdy*

- *Five-year guarantee*

Holding the Reader's Attention

The reader's attention is fragile and delicate. It is hard to attract and easy to lose—and there is considerable competition for that attention.

This is one reason why facts are so important and loose wording so deadly: the reader, consciously or unconsciously, resents wasting time on copy that does not describe, quickly and directly, benefits he can enjoy.

No thunks.

And no rattles, clanks, screeches, or hums either.
The new BSR 710 automatic turntable is designed to
be quiet, so you hear what's on the record, not
what's under it.

It uses a unique sequential cam drive mechanism
—an ingenious precision assembly that
replaces the plumber's night-
mare of rotating eccentric
plates and interlocking
gears that other auto-
matic turntables use—
light metal stampings
that can go hopelessly
out of alignment from
being carried, bumped,
or just from extensive use.

The 710 is reliable. Engineered to operate
flawlessly, and quietly, for years to come. If *you*
want to hum along with the music, that's fine;
but your turntable should keep quiet. The 710 does.
Write for detailed specifications to
BSR (USA) Ltd., Blauvelt, N.Y. 10913.

BSR

One of these ads combines a short attention-getting headline with persuasive copy; the other lets the headline make the sale.

Above all, give the reader facts. Writers of catalog copy, who are forced to cram all the pertinent facts about a product into a specific and usually small space, have the benefit of good training: when they find that their body copy is too long, the first words they eliminate are the puff words. Only hard, clean facts are left to sell the merchandise.

Be Human. Never assume that the reader prefers perfect textbook grammar to a few colloquialisms. This doesn't mean that copy should be overly folksy or slangy, which, as warned against earlier, is patronizing and phony; but writing in the same idiom in which people talk, without falling into the trap of sounding forced, can help avoid giving copy a coldness that makes the reader withdraw from it.

Be very careful that the copy doesn't become overly cute. The writer reaching for an identification with his readers too often ends up turning out trite, cute copy that fails.

Avoid Games. A writer of an ad can never assume that the reader will play the game the way the writer wants him to. A small ad was headed:

Feeling Blue?

If the reader says "no" to himself, he passes the ad by—and he very well may say "no," assuming that the ad is for a drug product or a loan company. Yet here is the copy that followed that headline, as it ran in a metropolitan newspaper:

Turquoise? Royal? Sapphire? Aqua? Dresden? Whatever blue mood you're in, the **** Company has the carpeting to match!

Imagine the readership that was lost because of an overly coy, inexact, nonmotivating headline.

Avoid Teasers. Another assumption that a writer never can make is that the reader is willing to study copy carefully to find out exactly what is being sold and how much it costs. A newspaper ad read:

Don't know what time it is? Your watch will do a better job for you after we have worked with it. For full details, write to: . . .

In the same newspaper, a competitor advertised a normal watch-cleaning and repair service at a specific price, and it is very probable that he got a better response. If an ad tries to entice a reader by saying, in effect, "If you ask me, I'll tell you what we're selling," the chances are the reader won't bother to ask. Teaser advertising works only when the product or service being offered is itself exotic enough, or new enough, or exciting enough to warrant such treatment.

Avoid Challenges. Challenging the reader of an advertisement can be dangerous. Too often, the challenge sounds to the reader like an order, and his instinctive response is rejection. Any headline that can be answered "No" or "None" runs this risk. Any headline that demands "Don't. . ." or "You should. . ." or "You shouldn't. . ." or "You'll be sorry if. . ." runs the risk of antagonizing the reader.

If hurling a challenge at the reader causes him somehow to feel guilty, it may turn him against the product. If it breeds hostility, it can antagonize him against the product. "Your next car should look like this. . ." proclaims a key color ad for a new model. The copy probably sold cars—but not as many as if it had not sounded to some readers like a command. How much more graceful, instead, to have said, "Your next car can look like this."

The Advantage of Being Concise

Good body copy, above all else, is concise. Conciseness does not mean the elimination of facts; it means the elimination of words that aren't useful to the impact of the ad. In fact, a good ad can have considerable body copy, so long as all the copy does a strong selling job. One of the most famous ads in history, The Sherwin Cody School of English's "Do You Make These Mistakes in English?" ran for nearly 45 years, earning its way each time. Yet the ad had hundreds of words. Another famous and successful ad, which ran for more than a generation, "They Laughed When I Sat Down to Play," was a solid page of copy, plus a coupon.

The key to conciseness in advertising and sales promotion is to get to the point quickly, make the point in clear and unmistakable terms, and then underscore it with all the facts that are pertinent. This approach is essential for a product whose use itself must be explained or shown, particularly during the pioneering phase of a campaign for a new product.

It is only slightly less important when the advertising for a product has evolved into a memory-nudging phase, after product identification has been achieved.

Offer Specifics.   The headline reads:

> *Broadway Motors proudly presents*
> *the greatest Chevy of them all!*

and the body copy reads:

> *We've seen 'em all before—beautiful cars with beautiful perfor-*
> *mance. But the new Chevrolet outperforms, outclasses, outbeauti-*
> *fies anything in its class. It's the car with the most, because it has*
> *everything. And it's all new, from the gleam of its front bumper*
> *to the flashing red of its taillights.*

Is it copy that is typical not only of automobile dealers but also of

This ad makes its point quick-
ly and reinforces it with perti-
nent facts—and no puffery.

many retail service organizations? Yes. Is it copy that can compete with tight, taut, concise, factual, descriptive advertisements? No.

Only those who believe in the "bulk theory" of advertising—that is, the theory that any advertising will succeed, no matter how mediocre its content, if it is repeated often enough—will consider such advertising valuable. Those who believe in such advertising also will say that it is superior to the kind of ad that damns the competition, which is true—yet couldn't the dollars spent for such an ad be put into a harder-hitting sales attempt? Couldn't specifics be given that would give the reader the motivation to buy?

In today's marketplace, where consumers in general have learned to beware, puff cannot be substituted for facts as a motivating force in copy. People simply don't believe that a product is "the best by far" or "superior in every way" or "incomparable by any standard."

Offer the Whole Story. Conciseness also means that nothing should be left to the reader's memory. The advertising writer should never assume that the reader remembers last week's or last month's ad. Every advertisement must stand alone in its ability to sell. While repetition does have its cumulative effect on the audience, only the advertiser with a mammoth budget can risk leaving any essential facts out of any ad.

Exploiting a Benefit

If a product does offer a specific benefit, exploit it, for it is an important selling point. If its benefit is obscure, or if the product differs only slightly from others, then concentrate on finding a sales appeal that will be attractive, logical, and unique in that no one else is using it.

> *A General Electric Potscrubber dishwasher*
> *is guaranteed to do this, or we'll take it back.*

The Danger of Attacks. As competition becomes severe and unique sales appeals hard to find, some advertisers, particularly on the national level, tend to substitute attacks on other products in place of beneficial claims about their own products.

Automobile manufacturers, for instance, often name each other in what they hope will be interpreted as "tell it like it is" ads. This is particularly true among the lower-priced compacts, whose attacks on each other can take visual form, even including "ours" and "theirs" photos in the same ad. The claim that usually is made is the more-for-the-money kind, often including a feature by feature comparison. This is a particularly fluid market, and manufacturers are scrambling for larger shares of the business.

Another particularly competitive field, and one rapidly running out of advertising themes because of the increasing pressure of attacks from various health organizations, is the cigarette business. Some companies have given up trying to suggest that smoking is a manly virtue or a womanly pleasure and are concentrating their advertising instead on their product being somewhat less unhealthy than that of their competitors. There is, for instance, the cigarette that has "less tar and nicotine than the best-selling filter king," a phrase that is tissue-thin under logical analysis.

Attacks can be dangerous, and the smaller the advertiser, the more dangerous his attack on another product can be. A giant automobile manufacturer, armed with engineering reports and a large advertising budget, can not only back up an attack but also handle it without causing a backfire. The Smith Drugstore, however, armed only with anger and a determination to get some of the Brown Drugstore's business, may find that its advertising attacks create sympathy and business for Brown's.

The Value of Truth. Does truth alone sell? Yes—if the facts given are stated in a positive form, and if those facts make a good sales presentation for the product.

Then what about those advertisers who decide, for its novelty value, to give the impression of listing faults as well as virtues? Such advertising may read, "Our competitor has new equipment and plenty of business—we have the desire to please you!" Or it may read, "Designed by Givenchy and Schiaparelli? Of course not. But these are carefully designed, well-fitting fashions. . ." Is such advertising successful? Very rarely, and it isn't anything for anyone other than the most astute professional to try. In general, advertising that concentrates on pointing out a product's deficiencies does an unselling job.

If a product's deficiencies are required to be mentioned by law, then the advertising must include the information. Cigarette packages now must contain a health warning, and medical advertising for drugs must include clinical information about any side effects caused by the particular drug.

This information is included, as required, and in the case of the drugs it may be a help to the doctor prescribing the product and thus a help to sales, but the information is not emphasized.

PUTTING STRENGTH IN COPY

Any basic writing course teaches that action words create better and clearer images and thus trigger stronger reactions than do passive words. "He walked down the street" is a simple statement of fact. "He trudged down the street" or "he skipped down the street" or "his feet flew down the street" or "he dragged his feet down the street" all present a much more vivid picture in the reader's mind.

Does this rule of writing apply to advertising and sales promotion copy? Surprisingly, not completely.

Advertising and sales promotion writing must be strong. Its job is to sell, and selling isn't an easy job. Being concise is important—and when that conciseness is given strength, then the writing can be very effective.

The deliberate attempt to be colorful, however, has ruined much copy. Color can confuse the strength of the copy. The druggist who featured a specific brand of aspirin with the headline, "For the lancinating pain of headache," not only didn't increase his sales, but even lost some, for the average customer associated the word with the discomfort of having something lanced. A slogan reading, "For those savage headaches when nothing seems to help," did far better. Strength in advertising writing doesn't come from colorful words—unless those words are concise and clear.

Words and Phrases to Use

Strength in advertising writing comes from reader involvement and the suggestion of something new or different. This is why advertising headlines that begin, "How you can. . ." or "How to. . ." or "Now you can. . ." have such strength. They involve the reader. They say, "This is you we're talking about, and we have something new to tell you."

In his book, *Confessions of An Advertising Man*,[2] David Ogilvy lists specific words that, he says, work wonders.

[2] *Ibid.*

The two most potent words one can use in a headline, according to Ogilvy, are: Free   New
Other powerful words and phrases are:

Suddenly	Sensational	Wanted
Now	Remarkable	Challenge
Announcing	Revolutionary	Advice to
Introducing	Startling	The truth about
It's here	Miracle	Compare
Just arrived	Magic	Bargain
Important development	Offer	Hurry
Improvement	Quick	Last chance
Amazing	Easy	

Note that each of these words again involves one of those two important ways to strength: reader involvement and the suggestion of something new or different.

The personal approach and newness plus exclusivity are excellent persuaders in a competitive situation. However, if the product is a new one, there must be a recognized competitive base. For instance, "New from Proctor and Gamble" is better than "New" alone, because the newness is tied to a known, accepted base. "Guaranteed by Wyeth Laboratories" may have only limited appeal in the consumer market, for the consumer may be unfamiliar with a name that is well known in trade circles, but "Guaranteed by Smith Drugstore and the world-famous Wyeth Laboratories" would get the point across to the average consumer, for the guarantee would then have a familiar base.

Other words that add strength are those the reader himself might use: "Oh, Honey, you brought me flowers!" has strength because the reader can visualize himself in this situation. The words "love" and "hate" both produce strong emotions, which can be used to advantage as in, "Hate washday? You'll love it with new Flash Detergent!"

Using strong words and phrases, it becomes easy to write acceptable, workmanlike advertising copy:

> *How to end your game of "detergent roulette"*

> *How to bring back the new white
> you thought your wash had lost forever*

> *Free! A whiter-than-white testing chart
> with new Flash detergent*

> *At last! The no-suds detergent that gets
> clothes clean quickly, easily, safely*

The words to beware of are often the superlatives. More than 30 years ago, motion picture advertising had already worn out the impact of such words as "colossal," "mammoth," "fantastic," and "magnificent." "Great" has no impact whatsoever. "Unique" and "unusual" are regarded as neither unique nor unusual. "Fabulous" has been so overused that it has come to mean "ordinary." "Wonderful" and "marvelous" have been used so often that they drain strength from the ad rather than adding it.

"Exciting" and "thrilling" still have some strength in certain kinds of copy, but the words generally have a feminine overtone. Imagine describing a man's after-shave lotion as "thrilling."

Try Negatives, Exclusives, Questions

Negatives also can add strength to copy: "You'll never have to worry about running out of gas again. . ." invites the reader to continue reading. However, negatives that suggest problems should be avoided: "No unpleasant aftertaste" implies exactly the opposite; "No long delays" has much less strength than "Three minutes—and your car is clean;" "Closed Sunday" has much less appeal than "Open every day, Monday through Saturday."

A feeling of exclusivity also can be a strengthener for copy: "Only at Smith Drugstore can you get. . ." has the power of offering the reader an exclusive opportunity. It has both the power of reader involvement and the strength of being a unique source of product information.

"You are invited to. . ." and "An invitation to join. . ." also have both reader involvement and exclusivity, for an invitation is an exclusive and personal thing. "An open letter to. . ." has the power of exclusivity, for the idea of a letter suggests something private, although even the most naive of readers would be aware that an open letter could hardly be considered private.

Questions have strength if they relate to individual wants and needs: "Are you still doing your washing the old-fashioned way?" and "Tired of fighting with a cold car every winter morning?" both suggest that the advertiser can provide a solution to a problem or a way of lessening the work involved in a tedious chore.

Identify With Care

One of the general rules of writing good copy, remember, is to be personal. The word "you" has enormous power. Yet it is also possible to be personal with the word "I." That personal touch, however, has to be handled carefully.

Such headlines as "Announcing with pride" mean nothing to a reader because they make no appeal to the reader's wants or needs. Yet the advertiser can use "I" and give strength to an ad, if his use brings reader identification without the embarrassment that the direct identification of the word "you" would bring.

One of the most famous mail-order ads of all time, "They Laughed When I Sat Down to Play," already has been mentioned. Not only did it contain considerable body copy, but it was written on an "I" basis. The ad succeeded because the reader could involve himself without feeling embarrassed; he could picture himself at the piano with his friends around him unable to believe that he could play so well.

"At 32, I thought I was washed up" is considerably more graceful than "At 32, do you think you are washed up?"—and, yet, the reader will get the point and identify himself without hostility.

What's in a Name?

Names, similar to descriptive words, can help create an image for a product or a company. The names to use in advertising and sales promotion are those that create the right image: An exclusive department store will have its store label, as well as the manufacturer's label, in all the clothes it sells, and it often will create original names for its various clothing departments. A budget store, on the other hand, often uses a brand name created for its image value, such as "Lord and Lord," in the clothes it sells. A cigar that had poor sales under the name "Long Boy" had a strong improvement in sales when one single change in promotion was made: the name was changed to "Imperial."

Automobile manufacturers, whose advertising often is pedestrian and bland, have accomplished much with names. There are many advertising experts who feel that a car named "Edsel" was handicapped to the point of failure by its name, while a car named "Mustang" was given a strong built-in boost towards success on the market. Automobile names that suggest speed and power are readily identified by the purchaser, who often refers to his car as his "Hawk" or "Cougar" or "Fury" or "Grand Prix" or "GTO," rather than by the manufacturer's name. Names that suggest status also are aids to selling: "Le Baron," "Bel-Air," "Riviera," "Fleetwood," and "Mark IV." That last has the distinction of sounding like a combination of a pope, a king, and an interplanetary missile.

Shortly after World War II, at the end of which the first atomic bomb was exploded, the word "atomic" was used to describe or name products ranging from gasoline to bubble gum. Then, "atomic" was replaced by "jet," as jet engines began to dominate the worlds of speed, power, and space. We have also gone through a cycle of names ending in "-rama" ("Colorama," "Futurama," "Powerama"). Right now, because there is so much talk about computers, there is a glamour in names that end in "-tronics"—so much glamour that some companies considering a public issue of stock believe that the stock will command a better price on the market if they add "-tronics" to their name in some way.

TESTING FOR EFFECTIVENESS

Even the most professional advertising and sales promotion writers are subject to a kind of ego evaluation of their own work. It is hard to spend hours, days, weeks, perhaps even months developing the words that go into an advertising and sales promotion campaign—and then be able to give a critical, unbiased opinion about the effectiveness of the words chosen.

There are three good ways a writer can test what he has done, even when his own opinion is too involved and too prejudiced to be trusted by himself:

1.   Get an outside opinion.

2.   Determine whether the copy achieves its goals.

3.   Test the copy for weaknesses.

1. Get an Outside Opinion

The best, the most unbiased evaluation comes from someone other than the writer. To assure the proper objectivity, that outside opinion should not be a general one but a specific one: anyone asked to comment on the theme, copy approach, or effectiveness of written material should not be asked, simply, "How do you like it?" but should be asked, "What is the most important point made in the copy?" or "How would you rate the message on a 'persuasion-strength' scale from 1 to 10?" or some other question designed to bring a detailed answer.

Such questions are not easy for the writer to ask of someone else. The less-than-professional copywriter, often a smaller marketer trying to put life into his business, may find such cold-blooded, objective viewing of copy over which he has labored so hard rather ego-shattering. However, it will keep him from wasting his advertising money on such useless headlines as:

Your success is our business

Pleasing you is our only product

The store that customers made famous

Such copy is typical of the noncommunicating, nonmotivating rhetoric that can slip past even the professional eye because it reads harmlessly but is a waste of advertising and sales promotion money. Such rhetoric transmits no message. It fails to sell.

"Your success is our business" is a line used by a national franchising company. It well may be intended to mean, "Our business is dedicated to your success," which is almost as dull and ineffectual. How much more potent the line could be if it were one of these:

Our business is making your business a success

We have never had a franchise failure

We don't make money unless you do—and we're making money

The basic idea hasn't been changed, but it has been made clearer and stronger by a more careful use of words.

2. Check for Goals

If the writer doesn't know a good outside critic, or if he wants a second check of the work, one way is to list the goals the written material is intended to achieve and then see whether it achieves them. This is a matter of determining what ammunition was going to be used, and assuring it was used.

For instance, a men's clothing store is having a sale of suits, and the department manager is asked to prepare a suitable advertisement. The goal of his ad is to sell more suits at a time when special low-price sale promotions normally are not scheduled. The ammunition he can use includes a 10 percent reduction from the regular prices, a full stock of current styles, a good range of sizes, and free alterations. In an evaluation of the headline alone, which headline would make the most impact?

1. *Suits, Suits, Suits—And What Values!*

2. *The biggest bargains in men's suits in town*

3. *For the suit of suits—Would you believe? A sale of sales*

4. *Next week you'll pay far more for each of these suits*

5. *Don't wait—buy now, and save 10% on every suit!*

The first headline is useless. It doesn't use the ammunition, and it doesn't achieve the goal. It fails to communicate anything that might motivate action on the sale.

The second headline is a cliché. It is a loose, unspecific claim without any facts backing it up.

The third headline is an attempt to be clever, and the attempt is made at the expense of the goal. That goal is to sell more suits, and there is nothing in the headline that encourages anyone to enter the store.

The fourth headline is the best one. It appeals to a basic human want, the desire for a bargain, and yet it does not cheapen the merchandise. It says "sale" without causing the reader to feel that the sale may be in a bargain store. It is the type of headline that encourages the reader to read on into the body copy, so that he can find out why the suits cost less this week.

The fifth headline probably is the one that would be most frequently used. It would have some success, but it also offers dangers. In today's marketplace full of advertising talking about "50 percent off" and "Save two-thirds of the original price," an ad that mentions only 10 percent and uses the weak words, "don't wait," simply encourages the reader to say to himself, "Why not wait? Maybe they'll come up with a real bargain. . ." It is a discount store headline without the ammunition of a discount store percentage of discount.

3. Test for Weaknesses

Someone writing advertising or sales promotion copy may be enthusiastic about the product; he may think he has communicated that enthusiasm by speaking directly to the reader, using "you" rather than "we"—and yet the copy may have dangerous weaknesses, which will lead to reader indifference.

A writer must always remember that he has a selling job to do. A reader doesn't aggressively or deliberately look for a specific ad; he will become interested in an ad only if the ad first demands and then holds his attention. A weakness in the writing can cause the ad to go unnoticed or can cause a reader to abandon it after glancing at it briefly.

Weakness in Comparatives and Superlatives. Comparatives that simply hang in the air with the comparison uncompleted, and superlatives that are not firmly grounded on an understandable base, cause a claim in an ad to seem generalized and weak.

Look at these comparative claims:

> *Flash detergent gets your clothes whiter. . .*
> (than what?)

This automobile uses less gasoline. . .
(than what?)

You'll save more. . .
(than what?)

Dentures will be held firmer. . .
(than what?)

"Whiter," "brighter," "longer," "better," "milder," "faster," "easier," "quicker," "farther," "tastier," "handier," "sharper," "stronger," "softer"—any ad that uses these comparatives to make a claim and fails to complete the comparison has what could well be a deadly weakness. People too many times have read comparatives that don't really compare; such comparisons no longer have any impact whatever and can even have the negative effect of turning a reader against an ad.

Superlatives also can be weak unless they are tied to a base that assures a specific reader benefit. Look at these wobbling superlatives:

The best shoes money can buy

The finest meal in town

The biggest buy of them all

Learn the latest from the greatest

Such headlines, some of which represent national advertising costing many thousands of dollars, are the result of assuming that people will be impressed by a superlative, even when that superlative is generalized, unexplained, and unfounded. But people are not impressed. Generalized, unbased superlatives result in another weak ad that lacks specificity, motivation, and credibility.

Weak Claims. Another test for strength in an ad is whether the claims made are backed up by facts. If the copy in the ad contains puff instead of fact, it fails to communicate. The generalized claim is one of the most common weaknesses in advertising. It results from laziness in determining what the true selling points of a product are and from a misunder-standing of why people buy, more than it does from an inability to write.

Typical examples of overgeneralized claims that affect credibility are:

Satisfaction guaranteed by America's
largest television manufacturer

Your satisfaction is our reason for
being in business

Where service is our most important asset

The place for fun

Once you try it, you'll never buy another brand

The ultimate in living room beauty

Advertising that seems stale and flat should be checked carefully for the weakness of the generalized claim. Brilliance is not required to remedy this problem: fresh thinking is. People cannot be bored into buying. A headline that reads, "Smart folks everywhere are shopping at Super-Marty's," is inferior in every way to one that reads, "Hey! We're having a ham sale and you're invited!"

WHAT DOES
THE CUSTOMER WANT?

Before putting any words on paper, any advertising or sales promotion writer, regardless of whether he is a professional or a merchandiser trying to work out his own ideas, should ask himself: "What does the customer want to know? What does the reader want to know? If I were buying, rather than selling, what facts, what arguments would convince me?"

Strength Sells

An automobile dealer tape-recorded the sales talks of his best salesman and his poorest salesman. He discovered that the difference was exactly the same as between a good ad and a poor ad: the top man used selling phrases that could have come from a good textbook in copywriting; the weak man made generalized claims that left potential customers unconvinced.

The rather unconvincing line, "A taste you'll long remember," was used by a restaurant that used small-space newspaper advertising. The owner couldn't afford to invest any additional money in advertising, but he hoped that repetition of the ad might build his image. What he overlooked was that the line was too vague, too generalized. He probably would have done better simply to have run the name of his restaurant.

An alert space salesman from a competing paper worked up a new minicampaign for him, using the same amount of advertising space but considerably different copy. The headlines began to read, "Why John Alva ordered two steaks," and then, "Mrs. Borne's third cup of coffee," and then, "The case of the undressed salad." It took only a few lines of copy per ad, but that copy was original; it reached for attention; it sold its product, the restaurant. Within a short time, the restaurant's business was going up steadily.

Exposure Sells, Too

A single running of one of the new ads might have won new business for the restaurant, but business probably would have slumped again if the small ad hadn't become a regular space-occupier in the newspaper. Except for the work of a very few advertising geniuses who combine remarkable imagination with unusual marketing expertise, brilliant copy seldom is an instant success. The goals are achieved by good copy and steady exposure of that copy to the public.

The ultimate extent of the success of a campaign depends upon the extent of the exposure that campaign gets. For example, suppose a small brewer in Santa Fe said to his advertising manager one day, "I have a great idea for a slogan. Listen to this: 'What'll you have? Brown's Best Beer!' " The advertising manager might have worked the slogan into a campaign, built around six billboards, a dozen radio spots, signs on the sides of the company trucks, and point-of-sale material for restaurants and bars.

Would the campaign have been successful? Within its very small radius, very probably so. In and around Santa Fe, people probably would associate the slogan with Brown's Best Beer.

But its effectiveness would be limited by the extent of its exposure, and "What'll you have? Brown's Best Beer!" would never be as well known as "Ivory soap, 99 44/100% pure" or "Ford has a better idea" or "See the U.S.A. in your Chevrolet"—or, for that matter, "What'll you have? Pabst Blue Ribbon!"

NOW, APPLY WHAT YOU'VE LEARNED

Test your ability to recognize and create effective advertising, based on the information in this chapter.

1. Select a consumer ad from your local newspaper; the ad should be coldly intellectual in tone, with no emotional appeal. Rewrite the ad, using the same basic information but switching the appeal to one that has an emotionally stirring headline and body copy.

2. From a trade publication, find an ad that is "we" in tone. Rewrite the headline, changing the "we" to "you."

3. Rewrite, for clarity and emphasis, this advertising copy for The First National Bank:

    Snug, secure, with the trust one can confer only to those whose honor is tradition-deep . . . your savings have found not a home but a nest, where they are pampered and caressed, to grow in an atmosphere of solid yet warm stability. Your father, your father's father, and your father's father's father before him, all may have helped found the inheritance which now is yours. And in a society which continually strips the warmth from the relationship between man and man, the subtle differences at The First have a greater significance than ever. Save at The First . . . where tradition is more than a word.

4. Select (a) a retail store ad, (b) a service ad such as for insurance or cleaning, and (c) an automotive ad, each of which has a noncommunicative headline. Rewrite the headline for each, adding strength by determining the goal of each ad and wording your headline accordingly.

5. You are one of five local dealers for the Automatique Self-Winding Watch. The manufacturer insists that each of you price the watch identically, at $145. All five of you will run individual ads in the local newspaper. Write your ad in a

manner that will give you individuality and dominance over the other dealers.

6. From a national magazine, select an ad that makes a generalized claim—an unexplained comparative or an unproved superlative. Rewrite the ad to make it credible.

7. For a computer school, deliberately write a pompous, "hifalutin" ad designed to attract students. Then rewrite the ad using a more direct aim at the potential student.

8. You market a brand of aspirin identical in every way (including price) to every other aspirin. Give your product a powerful name, and write a newspaper ad and a broadcast commercial that exploit your product's advantages.

9. You are the local Clearpix TV dealer. Your brand, in a color 22-inch size set, costs $35 less than the other major brands. However, it is imported from England and has no organized service-company arrangement, although parts and service are readily available. Write, first, an ad that tells the total truth about your product—the good, the bad, the indifferent, but the total truth. Then edit the ad, remembering that every word in your ad should be designed to make your product sell.

10. Using six separate words from Ogilvy's list, write six separate headlines to replace this one:

   "Make Cottrell's Your One-Stop Christmas Gift Headquarters This Year."

CHAPTER THREE

Designing the Printed Ad

Visual appeal adds power to an advertisement in a newspaper or a magazine. It is the appearance of the ad that attracts, that catches the reader's eye, that makes the reader stop to look. Even a powerful headline and brilliant copy often will be passed by, unnoticed, unless the visual design of the ad demands the attention of the reader.

The tremendous competition within printed media for the reader's attention has made eye-catching design mandatory. When the advertisement is placed in a newspaper or magazine, one cannot predict what adjacent advertising will look like; it often happens that the sedate, staid-looking ad is visually obscured by more dynamic advertising adjacent to it.

In the high-powered 1970s, boldness has replaced delicacy in most advertising. However, it is as true of advertising as it is of conversation that the person who shouts everything is "tuned out" and often not heard at all. Some advertisers believe that the way to avoid a too-quiet look is to load the ad with black type, black blocks, and screaming copy. The result is that by emphasizing everything, the ad emphasizes nothing.

Selective emphasis leads the reader properly through the ad. Part of the task of the layout man or designer is to create a series of visual impressions that not only gain attention but make coherent reading easy.

Only some high-fashion advertising retains the quiet, understated look that in many fields can result in an ad that passes unnoticed by the reader.

Imparting visual power to an advertisement requires a combination of mechanical knowledge and basic psychology. Here are the most important general dos and don'ts that make the difference:

- Do make the ad visually coherent; illustrations should reinforce and give added meaning to the headline and body copy.

- Don't try to emphasize everything. The beginner often believes that because every point made in his ad is important, every line should be given equal weight.

- Do consider using wide or tall illustrations and shapes: square shapes can be weak.

- Do use type to shout or whisper. The size and weight of the type should match the mood of the ad.

- Do ask yourself, when looking at the completed ad: "Have I captured, in picture and type, the flavor of what I am advertising? If not, why not?"

- Do remember that advertising experts know that they should appeal to the target readers and not to themselves.

LAYOUT

The term "layout" often terrifies the nonprofessional. It seems to imply exotic backgrounds in art and design and great creativity by expensive artists. Remember that good layouts can be simple—and that it always is possible to copy the look of a particularly attractive or eye-catching layout of another ad, changing copy and illustrations to fit the product.

While some of the artistic aspects of layout are indeed best left to the trained professional, the average businessman can learn enough to work out the simpler layouts and to explain precisely to a printer or an artist what is wanted in a more elaborate layout.

Formal Versus
Informal Layouts

First, imagine the beginning of the design of an ad as a blank piece of paper. On this blank piece of paper, which can be any size that an ad might be, are to go all the elements of the ad. Next, draw an imaginary line down the center of the paper, dividing the space in half vertically. There are two basic forms of layout, formal and informal. In the design of a formal layout, the elements of the ad are evenly balanced on either side of that imaginary vertical line. In an informal layout, those elements are unevenly balanced on either side of that line, creating a contrast.

Formal Layout. In formal layout, each element on the left is balanced by an element of similar weight on the right. That vertical line drawn through the center of the layout would find equal weight on each side of the line. The only variation possible is based on the seesaw principle: Just as a heavier child and a lighter child can work a seesaw by having the heavier child sit nearer the center, so can heavy and light elements of a layout be balanced on either side by moving the heavier elements toward the center of the ad.

One of the most common forms of formal layout is the use of a large photograph that occupies about two-thirds of the page. Below this, in a single line or two lines, is the headline; below the headline, the body copy is set in a neat block form. The large photograph catches the eye, and the overall look of the ad is dignified.

The photograph also could occupy about one-third of the space, but the effect would not be as eye-catching. What that photograph should not occupy is about one-half of the space, for one rule of formal layout is that an ad never should be visually divided into a top half and a bottom half: the two halves tend to pull away from each other, and the ad's coherence is lost. The two-third/one-third split is far more readable, more interesting to see, and stronger in its impact. (That the one-half/one-half split does appear repeatedly in both advertising and mailing pieces does not make it right.)

It might seem that formal layout is the best type of layout simply because it is balanced. However, that evenness of balance can drain emphasis and strength from the ad's impact. There are many uses for formal layout: in announcements, in institutional advertising, or in any kind of ad in which the advertiser wants to underline dignity and stability—but in readership tests, the informal ad often gets more attention.

Informal Layout. In informal layout, which is based on contrast rather than balance, elements of different optical weight are positioned at different distances from that imaginary vertical line that divides the space into

The Beosystem 4000
Fine instruments
for the reproduction
of music

A quality stereo system
must be much more than an
assemblage of components
that reproduce sound with
some degree of fidelity.
A system must also be
engineered so that all parts
function as an integrated
whole; the performance of
each component having an
exact relationship to that
of the others. This concept
of system development
finds apt expression in the
Beosystem 4000, a
selection of components
in fine balance, both
electronically and
aesthetically.

Bang & Olufsen
Excellence in engineering
Elegance in design
Two traditions from Denmark

Bang & Olufsen components are part of the permanent
design collection of the New York Museum of Modern Art.

Write for a brochure. Bang & Olufsen, Consumer Information, 2271 Devon Ave., Elk Grove Village, Illinois 60007

Courtesy of Bang & Olufsen

This advertiser uses a formal layout to emphasize the balance, both electronic and aesthetic, that he claims for his product.

An informally balanced layout can lend impact to an ad.

two vertical halves. One method of creating an informal layout is to position the elements according to the rules of formal layout—and then to move them deliberately into different contrasting positions. Good informal balance is harder to achieve than formal balance, however, since it takes an artistic eye to achieve a pleasing pattern. Too often, an attempt to create an interesting informal layout produces instead such a helter-skelter design that the ad is hard to read, or emphasis is scattered, or coherence is lost.

Color in Design

Because most printing paper is white and because the standard printing ink is black, any variation from the black-and-white look has attention value. An ad unread is an ad dead—and the gray look of a solid block of black type on a white sheet can be deadly. The use of color can add emphasis to an element of the ad through the obvious contrast between that color and the black and white areas around it.

Underlining or circling a word in color, printing an arrow or a price in color, or using a color as background for a block of copy or to give a rectangular shape to an illustration can draw the eye to an area of the ad that otherwise would lack strength. A solid block of color under the entire ad can give unity where none would exist otherwise.

The beginner often tends to overuse color. By remembering that in color, as in all other visual areas, to emphasize everything is to emphasize nothing, one can avoid a garish, undignified ad that lacks visual motion— that subtle but definite leading of the eye from element to element or the dynamic underscoring of areas within an ad.

The standard colors for printing (and when all are used, it is called a full-color or four-color process) are red, yellow, blue, and black. The first three are the primary colors, and thus the four colors of ink can be combined to produce any color, tint, and hue.

[Publications usually offer as standard second colors (in addition to black, which is the only standard first color in publications) red, blue, or green. Any other color is considered a custom color.]

Emotional Impact of Colors. Hundreds of years ago, purple was considered a "royal" color, because the deep purple dyes were so expensive that only royalty could afford robes of that color. Even today, the word "purple" has the sound of richness to it. Other traditional symbolic meanings of color:

> **White:** purity (sometimes coldness)
>
> **Black:** evil, death, judgment, authority, soberness
>
> **Red:** heat, passion, blood
>
> **Green:** nature, calm
>
> **Yellow:** sun, warmth
>
> **Blue:** loyalty, happiness, coolness
>
> **Gray:** neutrality, age

This is, of course, the way our culture sees these colors. Each culture interprets color in its own way. For instance, while white is the color of wedding dresses in this country, white is the color of mourning in India.

Visual Impact of Colors. The three primary colors are red, blue, and yellow. The seven basic colors of the spectrum are red, orange, yellow, green, blue, purple, and violet. These are strong, pure colors, any of which enhances a printed piece.

Modern psychology tells us that red is not, as was previously thought, the most eye-catching color. Orange-red is. For this reason, some manufacturers of fire extinguishers have begun to paint their product with this bright orange, since the eye goes first to this color. Ostensibly, if an orange-red color is printed on a piece of mail in the morning stack, the eye will go to that piece of mail first.

The greatest color contrast to the human eye is not black and white; it is black and yellow. Hence, many highway signs are painted in those colors. However, yellow and its adjacent colors should be used cautiously on light or pastel paper. For example, yellow letters on a white sheet of paper would be almost invisible.

Complementary Colors. Complementary colors are those at opposite ends of the color spectrum. Examples of pairs of complementary colors are red and green, orange and blue, yellow and violet. Since they offer the greatest contrast, they sometimes automatically are assumed to offer the greatest attention value.

However, the tyro who uses complementary colors of equal weight may create an unpleasant reaction on the part of his reader. Such colors tend to "vibrate" if placed together, causing eye fatigue. By mixing the hue of one of the two complementary colors to avoid direct opposites, a more pleasing effect will result.

(What's a good technique for determining the complementary color of any individual color? Stare hard at a swatch of the color for 20 seconds, and then look at a plain piece of white paper. For a short time, you should see the color complementary to the first color.)

Color Charts. It is possible to obtain the exact color and hue desired from any printer through use of the Handschy Color Chart, available from the Handschy Chemical Company, or the IPI Color Finder, available from Inter- chemical Printing Ink Corporation. These charts, which identify color chips by code numbers, have hundreds of shades of each color. The printer, told to match color CS-2504, can consult his own chart and mix inks according to a preset formula to produce that color.

Cost of Color. Each color adds 20 to 25 percent to the cost of the printing job. Is the extra cost worth it? Probably, if it prevents your advertising piece from having the nondescript appearance of "all the other ads."

However, there are ways of adding color economically: Instead of using full-color printing, the advertiser can give his ad or piece of direct mail the custom look by using custom second colors: metallic violets or rust browns, deep blue-greens, rich crimson reds. Lacking a Handschy or an IPI chart, the marketer can show his printer the custom color he wants by clipping a sample of it from a magazine or another mailing.

A three-color effect can be achieved easily by using colored ink on colored stock. Remember that the same color will appear darker on a light background, lighter on a dark background, and the same on a gray or neutral background. By overprinting the color on a light shade of black or by using different shades of the color itself, a multiple-color effect is achieved.

Methods for getting mileage from color are known to every printer. Many users of direct mail miss possible advantages because they fear their lack of technical knowledge. Your printer has that knowledge—use it.

Movement in Design

What causes the reader's eye to move from one part of an ad to another? Different shapes have different effects on the reader, either holding his eye on one spot or else directing it to another spot. A good layout is planned so that the reader's eye is drawn through the entire ad in a controlled sequence that should make the strongest impression on him.

The nature of our written language is such that we tend to read from upper left to lower right. That habit can be deliberately broken, if the

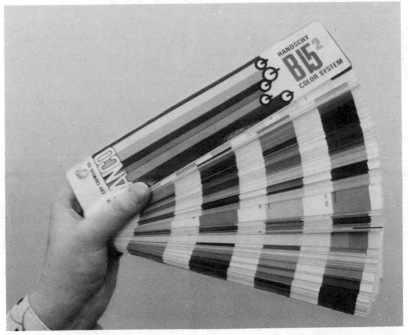

Courtesy of The Handschy Chemical Co.

Color charts show hundreds of shades of each color and make it possible to pinpoint the exact hue desired.

advertiser has a reason to lead the eye in a different direction. An arrow pointing at a particular block of copy will take the eye directly to that copy, regardless of where that copy is located in the ad. The risk, however, is that circumventing normal eye movement may cause some of the elements of the ad to be left unread.

An arrow is a direct command to the eye. This is why so many mail-order ads have an arrow pointing to the coupon. The eye follows the arrow almost automatically.

A circle stops the movement of the eye. Many retail stores whose strongest selling point is a low price will put that price within a circle, so that the reader's eye stops to study it.

A tall, narrow block leads the eye down, in somewhat the same way as an arrow.

Contrast in Design

Contrast of elements is an important way of catching the attention and emphasizing one point more than another. One basic use of contrast is within the copy itself: Initial letters (the first letter of the first word of a block of copy) or key words can be printed in bolder or larger type, thus drawing the eye to them. Alternating portions of copy, in which one paragraph is set medium face and the next boldface, adds readability and novelty, provided that the copy block is one that logically lends itself to this treatment.

White space around type adds contrast. One look at the classified pages of any daily newspaper will prove that the eye goes to certain ads, often because those ads use white space to break up the otherwise even grayness that causes the other ads to blend together.

In photography, the darker the background, the less that background will compete for attention with the foreground. This is a general rule that obviously has many exceptions, depending on the coloration or gray-scale of the foreground subject. Many black and white catalogs put the product for sale into a black or dark gray rectangle to prevent the other items that might be in the photographic field—even shadows or light areas—from attracting interest away from the central object.

Even a shadow can cause contrast; and contrast is not always desirable, especially if emphasis is lost through too strong a competing area of contrast within a single illustration. For this reason, photographic backgrounds may be retouched to eliminate contrasting shadows. Conversely, a thin shadow below a product may add strength to an otherwise weak pictorial image that has too few dark areas.

Background pattern and design can do much to emphasize a subject or to drain emphasis from it. If a background is exceptionally "busy"—for example, a strong geometric pattern, an optical effect, or a bright color—it can remove interest from the subject in the foreground. Photographic backgrounds that differ strikingly in color or tint from the subject in the foreground can produce strong emphasis, or they can create a split in emphasis by drawing attention to themselves if their patterns are strong or their colors are brighter than those of the subject.

Sometimes even a lack of contrast can have its effect. Fashion advertising sometimes deliberately and effectively flouts the rule of contrast. Some high-fashion photographers will show a model against a background in which the tone of color is almost identical with that of the garment being portrayed. However, it takes professional skill to handle the illustration so that the design makes the desired impression.

The question of background is one that has generated many arguments among advertising experts. Many say that showing a product in its natural background adds realism; others point out that the abundance of background details may pull attention away from the subject.

One compromise is to use the natural background but gray down everything but the product advertised. Thus, a dishwasher will be photographed in a model kitchen; then a sheet of "Zip-a-tone"—which has the effect of giving an overall gray look to any photograph or artwork over which it is applied will be positioned over everything other than the dishwasher. The effect is a gleaming dishwasher leaping out of its background. The same technique can be used to separate one building from others shown in the same photograph or to isolate one area of interest in a mechanical drawing.

The Design and the Product

The mood generated by proper advertising design can be tested easily: Using two fashion ads as samples, remove the price and the store identification. Almost everyone to whom you show the ads should be able to determine which fashion is more expensive.

The high-fashion look, as exemplified by the photographs in women's

fashion magazines, is unmistakable. The design is low-contrast; the pose is
artificial; backgrounds often are subdued. Budget fashion advertising, on
the other hand, is high-contrast and avoids the exaggerated postures, and
nondescript backgrounds. Artwork may be used instead of photographs.
Attention is to pattern rather than pose.

What makes people respond? Often, it is an appeal tuned to their image
of what the product might do for them. If a suit or a dress is shown in an
impeccable setting, with the high-fashion look, this alone is some justifica-
tion for a higher price.

How to Plan a Layout

That one need not be an artist in order to plan art treatment has been
proved so many times that it is an accepted technique among professionals
for a copywriter to draw, on a chalkboard, representations of the art he
might want—representations that are little better than the type of art one
sees in first grade.

What is important, in the planning stage, is not an appearance of
finished art but the positioning of elements. It is taken for granted that,
when needed, the art will be on hand, whether drawn to order or procured
from sources described in the next few pages.

Step One is to determine just what elements will comprise the advertisement or mailer. There probably will be a headline, perhaps a subhead, an
illustration, some body copy, a logo or trademark, perhaps a coupon, and
a border. One need not have even a sheet of written copy to plan the
appearance of the ad, although having a headline and copy makes the job
far easier.

Step Two is to decide on the position of the elements. A rectangle the
size and shape of the ad should be drawn. Then, using a pencil and often
actually avoiding a finished look, anyone can experiment. He can try a
huge headline, a normal headline, a diminutive headline. He can try an
illustration that covers the entire ad, with type laid over it; he can try a
high, narrow illustration, a round illustration, an illustration with vignetted
edges. (Vignettes have borders that gradually fade into white, so that there
is no formal shape to the illustration.) He can position body copy high or
low, to the right or to the left. He can have an idea of how a formal layout
would look, and he can try several types of informal layout. All this can be

done within a few minutes, since it is the positioning of elements that is being decided, not the design of each element.

After there is general agreement on the position of elements, then the nonartist can make up his own rough layout, indicating where illustration is to go, how much space is allocated for copy, and how large the headline is to be. From this, any layout artist can prepare his own rough layout for examination. And expensive art time has been saved.

Borders

A useful rule for the smaller advertiser might be: The smaller the ad, the bolder the border. Even a 1-inch ad can leap out of the page to attract the reader's eye when it has a heavy border on all four sides. Sometimes publications dislike using heavy borders on a small ad, and space salesmen, artists, and makeup men attempt to dissuade the advertiser either on the grounds that the ad will look strange or that it will look funereal. While they may be right, the advertiser's first loyalty must be to himself, and any technique that increases readership should be considered carefully.

Any ad that consists of a group of disconnected or unlike pieces should be enclosed within a border, for the border will add unity and help the ad be identified as a single entity.

Every newspaper and every commercial printer has a multitude of borders available, from plain rules of any width to such ornate effects as a line of stars or of holly leaves or of Greek designs or of interlocking spirals.

In larger ads, the choice of whether to use a border and of which border to use may be artistic rather than practical, for the size alone will tend to draw the eye to the ad. Often borders are not used in large ads. A full-page magazine ad, for instance, may use a "bleed" photograph, one that is printed to the very edge of the paper. Another ad design may be based on the white margins around the ad creating their own effect as a border.

A few suggestions about borders: A generalization might be that an ad that shouts demands a bold border, while an ad that whispers demands either an artistic border or none at all. Most newspaper ads need borders, or the ad may visually become part of the nearest strong ad and attract less readership. Sometimes it is a useful sales promotion technique to develop a unique border to identify a company's advertising or mailing pieces. Such

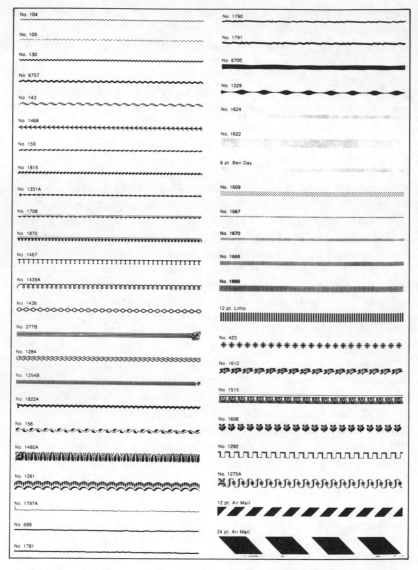

A border can unify an ad that is made up of disconnected elements. Newspapers and printers have a large selection of borders available.

a border might be the company name, endlessly repeated in a line, or a design that signifies the product or service the company supplies.

Reverses and Tint Blocks

Instead of black type or black artwork on a white background, a *reverse* uses white type or artwork on a black background. A *tint block* is a block of color or of gray on which type or artwork may be overprinted.

In general, the more dignified and classic an ad is to look, the less desirable reverses are. However, some highly sophisticated ads are total reverses: the entire art and copy are white on black. One objection to such a procedure is that it sometimes results in giving equal emphasis to every element in the ad, thus dulling the overall impact of the ad.

Reverses can be used as spot art in an ad. A retailer whose pricing is his strongest selling weapon might put those prices in reverse, perhaps white figures in a solid black circle or black rectangle.

Tint blocks are used in a somewhat similar way. However, they have a more dignified look than do reverses. Psychologically, tint blocks request attention, reverses demand it. (See illustration, page 89.)

GRAPHICS

No matter how brilliant the ideas, an advertisement is in danger of the damaging comment, "The thing just doesn't look right," if the illustrations used are poorly conceived or poorly handled.

The illustrations are part of the world of graphics. *Graphics* are the visual arts: painting, drawing, photography, and art design. Their execution involves professional skill and talent.

Yet, without an artistic background, a marketer still can learn enough about graphics to know how illustrations can and should be used. In addition, he can learn how to get what he wants and still stay within a reasonable budget.

Artwork: Help or Hindrance?

A question that always should be asked about any piece of art being considered for insertion in an ad is: Does this artwork help or hinder the understanding and the impact of the ad? Some advertisers subscribe to the theory that every piece of advertising should have an illustration of some sort in it, whether or not the illustration helps the ad, but this is a theory of dubious merit.

Ordinarily, pictorial treatment of any kind will help an otherwise colorless ad. It may be, however, that the art being considered is equally colorless and will add nothing to the ad.

Rather than insert a piece of art simply because it is artwork, the advertiser might try to determine whether the copy itself, or the typeface in which it is set, could be changed to accomplish the desired goal of increased eye appeal and interest. A simple reverse panel may draw more attention than an uninteresting piece of art.

Artwork: How to Find It

Because commercial artists demand a high hourly charge for the creation of artwork, and, more important, because communication with artists is not always satisfactory, the businessman should protect himself against the possibility of having described an art project to an artist and being presented with finished art that does not, in his mind, mirror his desires.

Art is a variable. Few artists will interpret a job the same way. For this reason, one of the most important initial steps is to request that the artist show his samples. The primary question, "What did this particular piece of art cost?" will often supply a yardstick that prevents arguments later on.

From an artist's samples, one can determine not only whether that artist is capable of the type of art desired; he also can determine whether the style matches the effect sought. At the same time, it should be remembered that the average nonartist should not attempt to impose too many restrictions on an artist; doing so will stifle any attempt to bring additional imagination to the finished job, and ultimately the entire creative process suffers.

Such types of art as product illustration, furniture illustration, fashion drawing, retouching and airbrushing, and architectural drawing, are all specialties. In the larger cities, each category may have many practitioners. But, as in any field, it often is true that the specialist commands far more for his talents than does the general practitioner.

The search for specialized art is not always profitable: The artist who does only architectural renderings may not, after all, be the man to illustrate a real estate ad. Conceivably, his art is too clinical, cold, and specific to sell homes through a newspaper ad. Or, his rendition may be truly beautiful in a large size and in color, but it may suffer in black and white, reduced for a small ad.

This is not to say that the specialists should not be used. Rather, their skills should be sought when the project warrants it.

There are, however, a number of sources of low-cost artwork, including several types of sources in which the finished product can be examined before it is purchased.

Artists. One logical approach for the businessman who has a fairly regular need for original artwork is to advertise in the classified columns of the local newspaper for freelance or part-time help. Those who apply will show their samples, discuss terms (whether by the job or by the hour), and give the marketer an opportunity to decide which style and price he prefers.

Occasionally, a local school will have either a student or a faculty member who can prepare the needed art. While such people are often a low-cost source of art, one should be careful and cautious in making arrangements with them. It is best to work with such people on a "payment on approval" basis until their work proves to be consistently satisfactory.

Whenever possible, one should try to negotiate a flat dollar arrangement for each job. This does more than pinpoint the cost; it also allows the

In this ad both a reverse and a tint block were used by the artist.

marketer to have minor corrections and changes made at no additional cost. Obviously, this does not mean that the buyer has the right to make arbitrary demands or changes in artwork.

Clip Art. A more economical but less individualized source of low-cost art is clip art. A number of commercial art studios have stock drawings, usually done in pen-line, that can be bought for one-time use for a flat charge. Or, one may buy perpetual nonexclusive rights. These drawings often are compiled in catalogs issued monthly, quarterly, or annually. A single purchase of clip art can provide a year's supply of usable art. Having the artwork available in advance enables an advertiser to tailor his copy to it if he so chooses.

Clip art is completely professional. In fact, some regular buyers are art studios and advertising agencies.

Since clip art is nonexclusive, one may run the risk of similar art being used elsewhere in a publication or in competitive mailings. As a practical matter this almost never happens; but some clip art houses will guarantee buyers that the sale is exclusive, either on a geographic basis or within a particular industry or business.

Whenever one uses clip art it may be a sound idea to photostat the art and use the photostat instead of the original. This assures the user of the availability of the same piece of art for subsequent use, without necessitating a search through old pasteups and advertising.

If the art contains a wash drawing or a photographic effect that shows subtle gradations of gray, it probably has been screened to the typical newspaper screen density—65-line or 75-line screen. (Screening is a process that converts gray and shadowed areas to tiny "dots" for printing purposes. Coarse paper, such as that used for newspapers, requires fewer dots because the spongy, absorbent paper may cause the dots to run together. A finer paper can take a finer screen—100, 133, even 200 lines.) Should the user want to change the size of screened art, he also will change the density of the screen, which may result in muddy or uneven reproduction in the ultimate publication. Thus, size changing is most simply done with "line" art that has no screened grays.

Since clip art is designed to have the widest possible use, it may be very general in theme. A marketer cannot expect to find his own product illustrated. However, it does provide very useful artwork for seasonal themes and for general use. Often, it can be adapted by a local artist for personal identification. Using clip art this way provides high-quality personalized artwork at a nominal cost.

Mat Services. Mat services offer the same kind of illustrations as clip art suppliers but in a form that can be used to prepare a printing plate. Mat services usually provide illustrations in two sections: They have a large volume of printed samples of art available and they also have rubberized cardboard mats of each piece of art, ready for use by the newspaper.

Most local newspapers subscribe to at least one mat service. Many regular advertisers also buy the service and then file the samples. Over a 2-year period, a monthly mat service will provide nearly a lifetime's supply of samples, provided that the art style and pictorial treatment do not become outmoded.

Mat services offer a considerable choice of seasonal material, since one of the main functions of the mat service is to enable the smaller newspaper to prepare professional-looking ads. Thus, mat art available for Thanksgiving ads may include illustrations of a large cornucopia and of turkeys of numerous sizes and appearances; line drawings of a family at dinner and a man carving a turkey; the words "Happy Thanksgiving" and "Thanksgiving Specials" in several sizes and styles; inspirational messages such as "Let Us Give Thanks"; art depicting hands folded in prayer, a child eating a drumstick, parents looking at a child and a dog playing—and perhaps as many as 50 other thematic approaches to the holiday.

Manufacturers. A source of artwork that is obvious and yet often overlooked is the company that makes or supplies the product or service that is being advertised. A farm equipment dealer, for instance, may find that his supplier has available many line illustrations and photographs of the equipment he is selling. Quite often, too, a supplier will prepare such art if asked. This art has the great value of being specifically of the product itself, something unobtainable in clip art or from mat services.

A Warning. Nonprofessional art users occasionally pick up a piece of art from an ad prepared by another company. Since this may well involve a violation of the copyright laws, it is not only unethical but legally inadvisable.

Photographs: How to Get Them

Photographs can be taken to order, by either the advertiser or a professional. They can be bought from stock suppliers, in much the same way as clip art is bought. In addition, there are many free sources of photos.

When ordering a print of a photograph from a professional source, one should always mention the use to which it will be put. This gives the supplier an indication of the tonal quality the photo should have—whether it should be "contrasty," with strong whites and blacks in it, or whether it can be relatively "flat," with emphasis on the middle tones.

Often, a nonprofessional will order a color print, even when he plans to use the photograph in black and white. Since the contrast ratio can be wrong for good reproduction, color prints should be ordered only when the reproduction will be in color.

In general, photographs for newspaper use should have greater contrast than photographs for magazine use. This is because newsprint, the paper on which newspapers are printed, is soft and absorbent. Its coarse fibers don't reproduce the delicate middle tones as well as does the hard, coated paper used in most magazines.

Photographs Taken to Order.   For the advertiser who wants to try to take his own photographs, here are several ways to achieve a professional look in photography:

- Try to have the lights high enough and the subject far enough forward from the background so that the shadows fall on the floor rather than on the background.

- Put a light above and behind the subject, a "rim light," to highlight the edges of the outline of the subject and separate it from the background. However, be sure the rim light does not shine into the camera lens.

- Even when shooting outside in the sunlight, it is a good idea to soften facial shadows either with an incandescent light or with a strobe light.

- A single light, aimed from camera position, will flatten and wash out details. A single light, aimed from the side, will emphasize textures, such as carpets, uneven surfaces, and serrated or curved edges. Lighting from right or left only and strengthening the rim light gives the shot an arty effect.

- For most purposes, a light-colored background is more pleasing than a dark background if the background doesn't compete with the subject in attention value. But if there is any doubt, go dark.

- A photograph of a product in use, or with a person somehow incorporated in the picture, usually is superior to a photograph of a product by itself—both in attention value and in psychological appeal.

A common error among those who take their own advertising photographs is an emotional one. The advertiser uses himself, his wife, or members of his family as models. Lacking the poise, and perhaps the appearance, of professional models, such individuals give an otherwise workmanlike photograph an amateurish look.

If professional models are unavailable or too expensive for the particular photograph needed, the photographer should take more pictures than usual, using more poses and positions than he might normally shoot. As is the case with portrait photographs, a multiplicity of poses gives greater assurance that one of them will show the subject to best advantage.

Although not generally accepted as professional photographs, Polaroid photographs have one advantage over conventional negative-produced photos: within a few seconds one knows whether or not he has the right shot.

Polaroid films have been improved, but the lenses on some of the less expensive cameras do not yet produce sufficiently sharp pictures. Nevertheless, Polaroids can be used for advertising and for news releases, and wider use is being made of them every year. Negative-positive Polaroid films permit multiple prints without a duplicate negative; high-contrast Polaroid films make possible unusual effects and easy duplication of charts and line art.

When taking a Polaroid shot for reproduction use, keep it on the light side rather than dark, and remember that there is less latitude for correction than there is with a conventional negative.

Even though the film package may indicate that an image can be achieved without professional lights, use flash bulbs or a strobe light to avoid that dark, unclear look that is characteristic of Polaroids shot indoors without this aid. As previously mentioned, even in bright sunlight a strobe will fill in harsh facial shadows, an aid even more important when shooting Polaroids.

Stock Photos. For pictures of the Eiffel Tower or a pretty girl in a bathing suit or a crowd of happy people or an auto wreck or a businessman behind a desk or carrying a briefcase or a trim young housewife winking or a cornucopia of fruits and vegetables or a druggist making up a prescription, stock photos are by far the most professional and lowest-priced source.

A number of stock photo sources publish catalogs illustrating some of the more popular photographs available from them. One-time-use rights to any one photograph will cost from $10 to $50, with $35 a reasonable average.

A look in the Yellow Pages of any large city phone book will show stock photo sources. Even without a catalog, photos can be obtained by writing any of the sources and describing the type of photo needed.

Selection of stock photographs must be made carefully. Too many stock photographs are entirely neutral in appearance, with no pictorial impact. This is because some sources deliberately deal in those photographs that are most general in appearance and therefore offer widest possible use. Their nondescript look lacks identification value.

There is one obvious advantage to the use of a stock photo: an advertiser knows exactly how the shot will look before he spends one cent. And there is one obvious disadvantage to the use of a stock photo: it is nonexclusive, and anyone paying the fee can use the same photograph (although, as with clip art, competitive duplication seldom happens).

Free Photos. Photographs of almost every conceivable subject are available free from a variety of sources. For example, beautifully photographed pictures of airplanes are available free from almost every airline—photos of trains from almost every railroad—photos of steamships from steamship lines—photos of palm trees and beach scenes from the chambers of commerce of many Florida and California cities—photos of factories from

Many stock photo sources publish catalogs showing samples of the photographs they have to offer. This page typifies the advantages and disadvantages of using a stock photo.

industrial sources—photos of college campuses and classrooms from colleges and universities—photos of city scenes from the chambers of commerce of many cities—photos of foreign scenes from the tourist office of the country involved—photos of automobiles from the manufacturers—and so on, ad infinitum.

Usually, the correct way to address an inquiry is to write to the "director of public relations" of a business concern or to the "director of information" of a nonbusiness organization.

Free photographs are no substitute for the professional shot-to-order photograph, but the quality of the photographs is excellent—and they are free.

When requesting free photographs, do not hide the use that is to be made of them. If the photos are to be used in an advertisement, explain this. This will save time and will eliminate the need to write again to get the proper permission to use a photograph. Ordinarily, use of a free photograph has only one requirement: that the name, if part of the photograph, be left intact (for example, the airline name on the side of the airplane) or that a small credit line appear beneath the photograph (for example, "courtesy of Florida Tourist Bureau").

Some sources that might not seem a ready or obvious means of obtaining free photographs become astonishingly cooperative when asked. A farm equipment manufacturer wrote customers asking for photographs of his product in use, with the customer in the photograph, and stated that these photos were to be used in advertising. He had a 20 percent return, and the photographs that were sent in ranged from Polaroid shots to large, expensive color prints.

Photographs: How and When to Use Them

Improvements in the lenses of cameras sold to the public and the rising wave of naturalism in illustration have combined to increase the possibility of photographic illustration in advertising and in marketing materials.

Indoor color shots remain the province of the professional, since only professional studio lights can assure proper color temperature and fidelity. But the huge 8 by 10-inch cameras that once made every shot a major production have given way to hand-held cameras that everyone can use. As the mystery disappears from photography, so does much of the cost.

Too much glamorous publicity has caused the average marketer to fear photographs. He visualizes a mad genius charging a thousand dollars for a single photograph of a gaunt female posed seductively beside his product.

There is just one determinant of professionalism in photography: If the photograph gets the message across, clearly and effectively, it is professional. Poor photos, on the local business level, are more often caused by an attempt to be clever than by low cost.

Product Photos. Photographs obviously are more graphically true than artwork, but the fear of cost and failure has caused many marketers to use artwork in their advertising and promotional materials even when art is less effective. In general, art sells a concept and photographs sell a specific.

The most simple promotional photo is the product shot. Retailers in particular and marketers in general usually can get professional photos of the products they handle from the suppliers of those products, as mentioned previously. These photos are usually available either in black and white or in color (and if the ad is to be black and white, get a black-and-white photo, for a color photo may lose much of its sharpness or have improper contrast in black-and-white reproduction).

Combining Photos. A steady hand and a sharp pair of scissors can turn stock photos and supplier photos into a promotional weapon that has a custom look. It is as simple—and as complicated—as combining the photographs so that they are more effective.

For instance, an automobile dealer may have many photographs of the current models he is selling. These photographs were taken by professionals, and few local photographers, without the involved studio and lighting facilities needed for these important product shots, could make the cars look as good. How can the dealer turn these good but bland photos into a meaningful ad for the local newspaper? He might well photograph customers who have bought cars and then combine the photos of those customers with the pictures of the cars. Properly handled, each will appear to be a single photograph with good local interest.

One franchising company has a stock photo of its principal officer, hand outstretched. When a local franchisee wants some publicity, he can have a photograph taken of himself, facing the other direction, and the two photos can be combined to make a single shot of a handshake for local newspaper use.

Travel agents have superimposed their photographs over foreign backgrounds, the combined picture underlining the theme that the agent can take you to any part of the world.

A Warning. Badly trimmed photographs that leave an uneven edge around the superimposed photo can have a bizarre effect. And the relative sizes of objects should be studied so that the result shows elements in their proper perspective. Otherwise, one runs the risk of ridicule from a photo that may show a giant beside a pygmy car or a tiny man next to a huge dog.

PRINTING

Printing, similar to graphics, often seems to be a mysterious aspect of advertising and sales promotion. Yet the technical aspects of printing are mechanical and logical, and it is easy to learn what is involved in printing and how to order printing work done.

The areas in which the average businessman is most likely to be involved are: choosing among the kinds of type available, choosing from the methods of setting that type, and choosing from the printing methods available.

Type

There are two basic families of typefaces: roman and sans serif. *Roman faces* are those kinds of type that have serifs. A serif is that little additional decorative line or cross stroke at the top and bottom of the alphabetic character. "Old Style" Roman has ornate, curved serifs; "Modern" Roman has flat or square serifs. *Sans serif faces* are the kinds of type without serifs. They usually have a more modern look, and the lack of ornamentation can make them highly readable, especially in the smaller sizes.

In addition, there are various special faces. Almost every typeface has a slanted variation called *italic.* There are scripts, which resemble handwriting in appearance, and cursives, which are similar to scripts except that the individual letters do not appear to be joined as they do in scripts. There are also highly individual faces, such as Wedding Text, Stencil, or Barnum, which tend to create a particular impression or mood or look.

The safest approach in choosing types is to use variations of a single face; this is called "monotypographic harmony." Most Roman and sans serif faces are available in lightface and boldface as well as the regular

8, 10, 12 Pt.   Monotype
Cheltenham Wide Italic   ! ? & $ 1234567890

18 Pt.   Monotype
CHELTENHAM OUTLINE   12

36 Pt.   Monotype
Chelt. Open 20

48 Pt.   Foundry
Chisel !?$12

18, 24, 30, 36 Pt.   Foundry
COMSTOCK ! $ & 1345

12, 14, 18, 24, 30, 36, 48, 60 Pt.   Foundry
Commercial Script !? $℣ 123456

8, 10, 12, 14, 18, 24, 30, 36, 48 Pt.   Foundry
Contact Bold Condensed   !? $ & 12345678

12, 14, 18, 24, 30, 36, 48 Pt.   Foundry
Contact Bold Condensed Italic !? $ & 123

24, 30 Pt.   Foundry
Consort Condensed !? $ & 12

18, 24, 30, 36, 48 Pt.   Monotype
Coronet Bold   !? $ &   1234567890

36 Pt.   Foundry
Cooper Blk.

8, 10, 12, 14, 18, 24, 30, 36 Pt.   Foundry
Corvinus Medium   !? $ &   1234567890

8, 10, 12, 14, 18, 24, 30, 36 Pt.   Foundry
Corvinus Bold   !? $ &   1234567890

Courtesy of Lakeshore Typographers, Inc. "A World of Type"

A single page from a typographer's catalog shows a sample of typefaces and sizes available to the advertiser. This page includes only those faces named from "ch" to "co."

weight, and many also are available in extrabold. Almost all are available in italic as well. Within a single typeface, therefore, enough variations are possible to give a lively look without garishness.

Except for fashion advertising, all advertising copy usually may be set safely in boldface. This is not a rule but a safety measure for the individual who is unfamiliar with the subtleties of type.

Type is measured in "points." There are 72 points to an inch. Therefore, 8-point type is 1/9 inch in height, and nine lines of 8-point type will be an inch deep. When set, however, type is often *leaded*, which means that an extra space is added between each line. To set type 8 on 10, or "8/10," means that 8-point type is being set with two points of space between each line. This book is set 10/12.

Standard sizes for type are: 5½-point; 6-point; 7-point; 8-point; 9-point; 10-point; 12-point; 14-point; 18-point; 24-point; 30-point; 36-point; 42-point; 48-point; 54-point; 60-point; and 72-point. Some faces are available in 120-point. Any size is possible, through photostating type to a larger or smaller size.

Typesetting

Few costs have skyrocketed over the past few years as quickly as typesetting. Despite this, some advertisers still blindly order type to be set, not knowing how it will look, not knowing whether it will fit the space available, and often without having considered alternative methods of having the type prepared.

Running an advertisement in the local newspaper is one good way to have type set free: most newspapers do not charge for type that they set for ads; instead they charge for the space occupied by the ad. By coordinating advertising and sales promotion efforts, such as scheduling ads to coincide with direct mail efforts, type that has been set, free, for the ad can give double value by being reused for the mailing piece. A newspaper will not object to setting up an ad even weeks in advance, provided the ad eventually does run, which allows the advertiser leeway in planning other uses for that type.

Multiple use of set type is an important reason why an advertiser should request proofs and mats of every ad he runs. These should be filed; for often, even a year or more later, much of the cost of typesetting can be saved by picking up what has been used before.

Hot Type. Hot type is type set on a conventional typesetting machine, usually a Linotype or a Ludlow machine. It is called "hot type" because the machine automatically forms each line of letters out of hot metal as those letters are typed on a typewriter-like keyboard. Since the invention of the Linotype in the late nineteenth century, this has been the standard method of typesetting, used by nearly all newspapers and magazines.

The setting of hot type is handled only by professional typesetters, those who work for publications or for typesetting companies.

Cold Type. Cold type involves no metal. Photocomposition, IBM typesetting, and Varitype are typical cold type processes. Setting cold type can be done by professionals, but some methods of setting cold type can be handled with reasonable success by the amateur.

For headlines, a kind of cold type involving "rub-off" letters has become popular. Some of the cold headline type brands available are Instantype, Artype, and Prestype. Each consists of groups of letters printed on transparent plastic sheets with special inks which, when rubbed with a stylus, can be transferred to a sheet of paper.

Using rub-off letters does require a steady hand, but it does not require artistic ability. Guidelines on the plastic sheets make it practical to construct perfectly straight lines. The average person can set his own display type using this kind of cold type, and it will cost him only a few dollars a sheet. Each sheet contains many letters, depending on the type size; there are many typefaces and sizes available. The disadvantage of rub-off letters is that the procedure does take time; for this reason it is not a practical method of setting body copy.

The Varityper is a machine with a keyboard similar to that of a typewriter. Unlike a typewriter, varityped copy can be spaced proportionally, enabling the operator to justify the lines; that is, make a perfectly straight right-hand margin as well as a straight left-hand margin. The resulting type image is clearer, sharper, and better for reproduction than typewriting, falling midway between typewriting and typesetting in professional effectiveness. Many typefaces are available for varityping, and these are quickly and easily interchanged on the Varitype machine. Such a machine is priced well within the means of a modest-sized company, and its operation can be learned quickly by any good typist.

The IBM Executive typewriter also has proportional spacing and often is used for preparing mailings and advertising pieces when the budget does not permit typesetting. While such a typewriter is limited to one size of type, it is easy to photostat the typed sheet to a slightly different size, thus giving it a printed look or else enabling it to fit into a specific space.

The IBM Selectric typewriter does not offer proportional spacing, but it does offer a choice of typefaces. It employs a type ball rather than the traditional set of striker keys. Many different faces are available, from scripts to Roman to sans serif faces, and the type balls can be changed in seconds. Typing on a Selectric typewriter is not intended to replace professional typesetting or varityping, but it can be used for low-cost reproduction, and changing the type ball can give a typeset look to a sales letter, enabling the emphasizing of one paragraph, for instance, by the use of a different typeface.

IBM also leases or sells a cold typesetting machine. The keyboard is identical to a standard typewriter, but the typesetting machine justifies both left- and right-hand margins, has proportional letters and spacing, has many typefaces of varying appearances and weights, and also offers options of a number of type sizes, ranging from 6 to 12 points. For the company using the machines there is a basic monthly rental charge; beyond that, typesetting costs little more than straight typing. The IBM typesetter has been especially valuable to companies that want professionally set bulletins, brochures, and mailing pieces without paying outside typesetting charges.

To obtain the best reproduction from any cold type method, never varitype or typeset on soft paper such as bond. Use coated or enameled paper to get the sharpest possible image. Soft paper acts like a blotter for the ink, while hard paper keeps the image crisp. (This suggestion has nothing to do with the paper on which the job eventually is printed but refers only to the paper containing the type that will be pasted into position for platemaking or photography.)

Fitting Type Into Space

What size type should one use? If there is no problem fitting the set type into a specific space, the easiest method is to indicate type by drawing letters of the size wanted as a yardstick to the typesetter. He in turn will select a size that most clearly matches the indication.

Many who are not totally familiar with the graphic arts do not realize that within a given type size, italic or boldface type occupies exactly the same amount of space as the medium face of the same size. It is when a condensed or expanded version of a typeface is chosen that the number of letters that will fit within a line changes.

The most basic use of a knowledge of type fitting is in the classified ad. Instead of 6-point or 12-point type, many newspapers indicate classified faces as "No. 1" or "No. 2." No. 2 may be the same face as No. 1 but will be twice as large.

The logical method of determining how much space is required for the message that is to be set is to measure the average number of characters in a line. Suppose, for example, that the chosen face averages 34 characters in a line 2 inches wide. By setting the typewriter margins 34 characters apart, the typed copy will give a close approximation of the number of lines required.

If, when typed, there appears to be too much copy for the space, there are three solutions: (1) allocate more space, (2) cut copy, (3) set the type in a smaller size. If, on the other hand, the copy does not occupy all the allotted space, one can add space between paragraphs or between heading and body copy.

Six lines of 12-point type, set "solid" (with no additional space), will be an inch deep: as previously mentioned, there are 72 points to an inch, which makes 12-point type 1/6 inch deep. But those same six lines of 12-point type, set on 14 points (that is, "leaded out" two additional points between each line), will be an extra 10 points deep.

Another method of type measuring is the square inch technique. This method is far quicker (although less accurate) than the average line method.

Typefounders long ago established a table that averages the number of words per square inch of type set solid:

Type Size	Words per Square Inch	Type Size	Words per Square Inch
5 point	69	9 point	28
5½ point	65	10 point	21
6 point	47	11 point	17
7 point	38	12 point	14
8 point	32	14 point	11

Since type increases in size geometrically rather than arithmetically—that is, 14-point type will be far more than twice the size of 7-point type—it never should be assumed that using a size half as large as another size will result in a type block only half as large.

How does one use this table? If there are 600 words and the allowed space totals 2 inches by 5 inches—or 10 square inches—a safe bet would be 6-point type (470 words), leaded out for easy reading.

As a general rule, body copy should not be set larger than 12 points. But, as is true with almost any rule, this one has many exceptions. Another general rule might be that only copy that is assured of readership without having to sell itself visually should be set solid in a small size.

Printing Methods

The two printing methods most likely to be encountered by the average businessman are letterpress and offset. *Letterpress* is the process that uses raised letters inked by rollers to print an image on the paper. *Offset* is a process that uses photographic plates, treated so that different portions retain different amounts of ink spread by rollers, to print the image on the paper. Offset, in its simpler forms, costs much less than letterpress, although the more elaborate kinds of offset equipment can be just as expensive or more expensive.

Planning Printing. The most common standard size of printing paper is 17 by 22 inches. If a marketer is planning an ad for a publication, paper size is not important to him—but if he is planning a printed mailing piece, paper size can make a big difference in cost. Paper is expensive, and its price keeps going up. A mailing piece should be planned so that its size avoids paper wastage: four 8½ by 11 sheets can be cut from a master sheet of 17 by 22 inches, but only two 9 by 12 sheets can be produced, causing considerable waste.

It is the makeready or preparation for the press run that costs the largest proportionate amount of money. Once the presses are running, the cost per copy drops considerably. Thus the cost per piece of printed matter declines far more sharply with increase in quantity than almost anything else a marketer buys. An extra thousand copies may require only a few minutes of press time and a few dollars' worth of paper.

Thus, in planning printing, it is wise to determine the maximum number of copies that might be used. However, don't pad this figure, for paper does cost money, and unused copies are a waste.

Plates and Mats. For letterpress jobs, and for most advertisements that are run in newspapers or magazines, printing plates are prepared. For newspapers and short pressruns, "stereotype" plates made of lead are used; the more expensive copper or nickel "electrotype" plates are used for longer runs and better-quality printing.

When similar ads are to be run in several publications, it is practical to have mats prepared. *Mats,* which cost only pennies in comparison to the many dollars plates cost, are cardboard impressions of the original plate. Sent to another publication, the mats serve as a mold that is filled with hot lead to prepare the equivalent of a stereotype plate. Newspapers ordinarily make no charge for casting plates from mats.

Printing plates made of plastic increase in popularity each year. They no longer are considered experimental. Less expensive and lighter in weight than metal plates, they offer better quality than mats, especially in reproducing photographs.

Printing Negatives. Offset publications use photographic-type negatives rather than plates. These negatives are made by photographing clean ("etch") proofs of the finished pasted-up job.

A good printer will know how to match paper, color, coarseness or fineness of screen, size, and type to provide a professional, interesting-looking finished printed job.

NOW, APPLY WHAT YOU'VE LEARNED

Test your ability to use simple design tricks to get attention, based on the information in this chapter.

1. From last Sunday's newspaper, select an advertisement that has little visual power. Using the rules for creating a visually powerful ad, indicate a new layout. Do not change copy or drop any elements; your job is to keep everything but re-arrange for greater visual strength.

2. Find an ad that seems weak because of its border. Clip a border that fits the mood of this ad from another ad or source and carefully affix the border to the ad.

3. Choose a full-page magazine ad in which the layout is static. Rearrange the layout for greater force.

4. Choose two full-page magazine ads. One should have formal layout, the other informal. Make new layouts for each ad; arrange the formal ad in an informal layout, and arrange the informal ad in a formal layout.

5. From a magazine, clip samples of ads that use these families of type: old-style Roman, modern Roman, sans serif, italics of each of these, script or cursive, a special or exotic type-face, and handlettering. Evaluate each ad in terms of the appropriateness of the type style.

6. Without using a photograph of a hairstyle, suggest three illustrations for an ad for Genie Hair Stylists.

7. Pretend that today's newspaper is a stock-art or mat service. You may use any piece of art in the paper, to help you build a 7 x 10-inch ad (with coupon) for a trade magazine in which you will advertise your product: AUTOMATON, an auto-matic unit counting machine for any business requiring a production line. You decide what the ad should say; the coupon is for additional information. Remember that three competitors also will advertise in this trade magazine, which

means that your headline, layout, and illustration should generate interest and blaze with power.

8. Using basically the same materials, design a second ad for the following issue of the trade magazine. Save money by picking up what you can; but the ad should NOT look identical or cause a reader to feel that he has seen this ad before. You are after maximum effectiveness at the least mechanical cost.

9. From an art store, obtain a sheet of cold headline type. Set this headline, to appear in a 7 by 10-inch ad:

Is There a Branch Bank in Your Home?

10. Write total copy to fit the rest of the ad, and suggest photo or artwork. [The bank is (your name) Bank.]

CHAPTER FOUR

Direct Mail and the Broadcast Media

In terms of total expenditures, more money goes into print than into any other advertising medium; television is second, direct mail third, and radio advertising fourth. (Advertising placed by the advertising giants is responsible for boosting television into second place. Smaller marketers often put direct mail in a prime position; in fact, direct mail is the only medium used by many small companies.) The latter three media will be the subject of this chapter.

Traditionally direct mail has been an important advertising medium for most marketers, and it remains in first place for some marketers today. A look at the content of a typical day's mail proves this: ads often outnumber personal communications. Because the mailbox has become so crammed with mail and because the cost of direct mail is higher per capita than that of any other mass medium, today's marketer must put more skill than ever into his mailing piece so that it demands and wins attention.

When commercial radio stations began mushrooming in the 1920s, radio commercials grew right along with them. The popularity of radio as an advertising medium continued until the early 1950s, when television began its ride into popularity—but after several uncertain years, radio advertising revenue increased again, thanks in part to the transistor radio and the huge automobile-riding audience. National advertisers have put considerable money into national spot campaigns, while smaller marketers have found local stations profitable ad carriers.

Radio was the first mass advertising medium to allow marketers to talk about their products, not just write about them. Then came television, which enables an advertiser to use both sound and a visual image to do his selling. Television is fascinating—and expensive. However, while the larger companies account for the major expenditure in television advertising, smaller companies are learning that economical ways of cashing in on the drawing power of this newest medium exist for them.

DIRECT MAIL

Visualize the typical businessman attacking his mail on a typical day. That mail consists of 10 to 30 items—envelopes and cards of many sizes and colors. Some pieces are tossed unread and unopened into the wastebasket; some are given a quick look and then discarded; some are placed aside for more intensive scanning later; some are read on the spot.

How can your mailing piece qualify for those elusive, elite last two categories? If there is a one-sentence rule of how to stay out of the wastebasket, it is: On both the outside and the inside of the mailing piece, create the impression that you have something to say that the recipient wants to know.

The first hurdle a good mailing piece must overcome is to convince the recipient to open the envelope. Once the envelope has been opened, then the number of items within that envelope, the way color has been used, and the way the covering letter has been handled all will help determine the impact of the advertising message on the recipient.

Choosing the right mailing list is important. So is thoroughly under-standing Postal Service regulations. Most important in an era of rapidly rising costs is knowing how to accomplish an effective direct mail job as economically as possible.

Today's typical mailing consists of four or five pieces: an exciting envelope, a covering letter, a piece of literature (folder, flyer, broadside, or brochure), an order blank, and a business-reply envelope (these last two sometimes combined in a single piece).

An Irresistible Envelope

A third class mail envelope, on the face of which is printed the company name and address, the recipient's name and address, a third class mail permit number, and nothing else, shouts that it is unsolicited mail—and most of us are geared to ignore or reject unsolicited mail. The outside of the envelope is the original motivator; it should make the recipient want to look at the contents it holds.

Try using one of these strong pullers on the envelope. The power of a single sentence can be surprising:

- Immediate Reply Requested

- Dated Material—Do Not Delay

- Confidential Information

- Do Not Forward to Anyone Other Than Addressee

- Please Read at Once—Valueless If Delayed

- Private Offer for Addressee Only

- Personal (still the most potent of all)

Use the good ideas others have, too. Start now to collect all business mailings you receive in which the approach seems fresh and attention-getting. When the time comes to prepare your own mailing, one of these samples can help, not copied but used as a spark for an original idea of your own.

The Covering Letter

The key component of the direct mail piece is the covering letter. This is the personalization that makes sales literature credible—or incredible.

The impact of a professionally written sales letter depends neither on a massive command of vocabulary nor on slick trickiness. Rather, it depends on an impression of sincerity, truth, and believability.

Professionalism in sales letters is simple, if you use these basic techniques of good letter writing:

- Keep your first sentence short. The involved first sentence has killed off more readers than any other pompous device.

- Forget the generalized, impersonal greeting. "Dear Sir," "Gentlemen," and "Office of the President" depersonalize your letter and damage the effect you are trying to create. If you cannot afford the standard "Dear Mr. Smith" because of the cost of hand typing, try something like this: "Memo to Buyers of Insurance" or this: "A personal message to a favorite customer."

- Allow no paragraphs longer than seven lines. The recipient of the letter decides at a glance whether or not he will read it. If he sees a gray mass of forbidding copy, he may decide against it. Short paragraphs give the reader "absorption time," which means not only a better reception to your message but improved comprehension of it.

- Avoid clichés and lazy generalizations. You're deader than a doornail if you lead with your chin instead of putting your best foot forward. (Reread this sentence: three clichés in a neat, dead row.) Clichés represent laziness of thought, an unwillingness to visualize and create exciting word images. The one sure way to avoid clichés is to reread the letter before final typing with the single aim of destroying any clichés that have sneaked in.

- Load the letter with "you," not "I" or "we." The letter that begins, "We've developed a new machine that outclasses all others in its field" is inferior to "You'd have time for an extra nine holes of golf every afternoon if you owned this machine" because the "you" makes the reader identify with the benefit.

- Wide margins are more effective than double spacing. When you have a short message, the letter will read better if, instead of double spacing to use up more of the page, you leave wide margins and double space only between paragraphs. This is another way of avoiding the gray look that makes a letter a candidate for the wastebasket.

- Forget that the phrase "Yours truly" ever existed. In a sales letter, why not let the close add a little more sell? Instead of "Yours truly," try something with impact: "Yours for better

The unsolicited mailing piece that is not tossed unopened into the waste-basket is one whose envelope tells the recipient that it contains something he wants to know.

profits" or "With every wish for your success" or "Frater-
nally" or, if the letter is a formal one, "Sincerely."

- Fire your biggest gun first. Every letter writer likes to drama-
  tize—but, unfortunately, the number of master storytellers
  among sales letter writers is not significantly high. Don't take
  a chance. The reader has neither the time nor the patience to
  hunt for your point, brilliantly buried in the seventh paragraph of your letter.

To Cram or Not to Cram

"You can tell when a mailing has been prepared by an old-timer," the head
of a mailing service said. "It has a million pieces."

Forty years ago, when a lot fewer mailings were being made and the
Sears, Roebuck catalog was the highlight of the season, readership was
more intense than it is today in the multimedia 1970s. The time a

Allstate

375 South Washington Avenue
Bergenfield, New Jersey 07621

Leo A. Bottari
Senior Account Agent

Been bitten by the New-Car Bug?

Be sure to figure out the finance charges before you sign. You may be able to save up to $100, or maybe even more, by financing your next car through Allstate Econo-Rate* Finance.

Besides the economy of low finance charges, Allstate offers the speed and convenience you want. In most cases, with established credit you can arrange for your financing and have a draft to pay the auto dealer the same day. It's even simpler if you want to complete the Econo-Rate credit application ahead of time. Your credit identification will let you pick up a draft without further credit reference in a matter of minutes ... anytime within a six month period.

You can handle the application by mail ... no "trip downtown" needed. Just fill out the enclosed credit form and mail it to me now, even if you don't plan to buy your car right away. Or contact me if you have any questions about auto financing.

Remember, if you're in the market for a new car, you look for the best possible deal. I think you'll find Allstate Econo-Rate Finance is your best deal for a low finance charge plus convenience. Mail the credit application, today!

Your Agent
Allstate Enterprises, Inc.

MFDAC:B.
Enc.

Does this cover letter fulfill the basic requirements for a professionally written sales letter? Is there a sentence within the letter that would be a better first sentence?

recipient used to spend with a mailing often was proportional to the size and content of that mailing, which meant that a thick mailing commanded more time and more attention. Today, with television viewing having replaced mail reading as a prime evening activity and with an increase in the amount of mail received both at home and in the office, it is obvious that a direct mail piece commands less attention.

However, some of the giants in direct mail regularly use thick, heavy mailings, reporting that their volume drops proportionally with a reduction in weight or number of enclosures. One company that uses direct mail to sell men's ready-to-wear stuffs each envelope with 20 or more small descriptive sheets (unbound, to make reading and saving of an individual sheet easier) plus samples of fabric, free offers, and discount order coupons, a total of 30 or 40 separate items.

Within its own framework, the old-time philosophy of "cram the mailing!" seems to work. A mail-order pioneer who has never varied from this formula has said that he tells it to them, then tells it to them again, and then, after they've picked up what seems to be the hundredth piece of paper, there it is again. He contends that there's nothing wrong with repetition—it makes the reader feel secure. He repeats the same offer over and over and the reader is sure to understand it.

Deciding whether to cram or not to cram depends on:

- The budget available

- Previous experiences with similar mailings

- What is being offered

The budget determines what can be spent, and every additional item in an envelope means an additional cost both in preparation and in postage. Previous experience with similar mailings may show that a crammed envelope has done a good job in the past, or it may be that such mailings did not pull sufficient response to justify the expense. And while some offerings can be handled very well by multiple enclosures, others cannot. That marketer of men's ready-to-wear found it profitable to list each style available on a separate enclosure, but a marketer selling a line of motorcycles probably would find a colorful brochure or booklet more effective, since models can be compared with each other with greater ease and the overall look is one of better organization.

Reader-Involvement Enclosures. Since psychologists teach that involvement breeds action, the most alert users of direct mail usually have at least one enclosure that gives the recipient something to do: He is asked to paste an enclosed stamp in a specific area of the business-reply card. He is asked to check "yes" or "no," which does not affect his chances of winning a prize but does get him involved. He is asked to provide the date of his birth or the make and model of his car or his profession. He may even be asked to remove a penny or a dime, which is his to keep.

Such enclosures may be "hucksterish," but they can disarm a doubting recipient. One good enclosure is a foil-wrapped individual serving of coffee, with a letter that states, "Let's discuss this over your morning cup of coffee." Two aspirin in a glassine sleeve inspire this one: "Do (names of problems) give you a headache?" A dime pasted to the letter might be accompanied by, "I have an investment in you," or to a local account, "Call me—it's my dime."

In each case, because he has done something, because he has become involved in some way, the recipient probably will remember the mailing longer and may act on it.

Postage-Free Replies. Most users of direct mail still enclose postage-free envelopes, knowing that the use of such envelopes increases the pull of the mailing sometimes by hundreds of percents. A trend, begun in the late 1960s because mailing costs had become so high, has become the "affix stamp here" concept.

The "you pay the postage" idea has gained favor in circumstances in which the recipient of the mailing obviously has more to lose than does the mailer if a reply is not sent. For instance, a particularly attractive offer may be available only if the recipient fills out the order form—and puts a stamp on the return envelope.

Coupons in Ads and Mailing Pieces

As a rule direct mail pieces ask for action on the part of the reader. Coupons often are used to make it easier for the reader to act. Coupons are used in newspaper and magazine advertising for the same reason. If action by mail is the intent of an advertisement, tests have shown that the incorporation of a coupon in the ad can increase readership responses by 100 to 300 percent.

American Traveler

Abercrombie & Fitch
Madison Ave. at 45th St.
New York, N.Y. 10017
Dept. 41 and 60. Please send me:

Quan.	Item	Color	Size

Charge my A&F Account # _____
Charge Master Charge # _____
Charge BankAmericard # _____
    Expiration date _____
☐ Check or ☐ Money Order enclosed.
Please add sales tax where applicable.
Beyond delivery area, add 1.10 for shipping
and handling.

Print name _____
Address _____
City _____ State _____ Zip _____

Shop easily and quickly with your
Abercrombie & Fitch Charge Card,
Master Charge or BankAmericard.

ABERCROMBIE & FITCH

Gleneagle...
the ideal raincoat
Finest polyester/
cotton poplin, with a
warm but lightweight
zip-out wool lining.
Take it with you
wherever you go!
In bamboo. Sizes
36-48 R, 36-42 S,
38-46 L. Even
sizes only. **$80**.

ABERCROMBIE & FITCH

*Courtesy of Abercrombie & Fitch,
New York, N.Y.*

(Above) *A retailer often adds
enclosures to his monthly bill
which describe items he has available and provide a form for convenient ordering.* (Left) *Coupons
make it easier for the reader to
act. They also tell the reader that
his inquiry is solicited and wel-
come.*

Responses to ads with coupons are useful to advertisers in building their mailing lists. When an advertisement asks the reader to fill out and return a coupon to obtain more information, the advertiser follows up with a direct mailing; and the respondents are added to the mailing list.

A coupon has to be considered when one is preparing the layout of an ad, for it is an important element in that ad. A reader service card (see page 119) is not physically a part of the ad, but when a publication offers the use of a reader service card, it is useful to find out what code number the publication intends to use to designate the ad on the reader service card and to make sure that that number is incorporated in some logical position in the ad. Sometimes that position is determined by the publication, but often it can be chosen by the advertiser.

The advantage of a coupon is that it makes an ad easier to answer. It also clarifies the requested action for the reader. In addition, by involving the reader, by giving him something to do, rapport is built.

The negative aspect of coupons is that they tend to weaken the ratio of inquiries to sales. As one old-time mail-order advertiser explained, "When I run an ad without a coupon, I get 10 inquiries and make 5 sales. With a coupon, I get 30 inquiries, and if I'm lucky, I make 8 sales." Unquestionably, a coupon does bring in some inquiries from people who are only vaguely interested, but it is the job of the salesman handling the follow-up to convert casual interest into sales.

If orders rather than inquiries are the goal, with the reader expected to send money in with the order, then a coupon is a must.

Designing a Coupon. Too many small advertisers decide to use a coupon without making any adjustment other than tightening the ad to make space for the coupon. The result is that not enough room is allowed for the coupon. A coupon that does not have sufficient space for name, address, and ordering instructions may work against the advertiser, not for him. Most people can remember at least one instance of clipping a coupon from an ad, trying in vain to squeeze in a name and address, and then giving up in disgust.

A dotted line usually is used to box in the coupon. Perforation increases the ease of use.

Placing the Coupon. Traditionally, coupons are placed in the lower right-hand corner of the ad. Some advertising men have claimed that since an ad with a coupon is designed to convince people to use that coupon, the coupon should be placed at the top of the ad where it would be more prominent, more noticeable, and therefore more likely to be used. A disadvantage of putting the coupon at the top of the ad, however, is that because of the natural movement of the eye, the coupon is seen and passed by before the reader knows what the ad is about.

One of the most common reasons for the failure of a coupon is the advertiser's lack of control over what appears on the reverse side of the page. While publications try never to place two ads with coupons back to back, this does happen occasionally, and both coupons might represent products or services interesting the same reader. If the other side of the page has editorial matter on it, often a reader will delay tearing out a coupon, thinking that he will come back to it after he has finished reading the publication. The majority of readers never do turn back to retrieve that coupon.

This, plus the novelty value of the idea, has prompted some advertisers to buy the space on the page behind the coupon. The ad itself may be a full page, with the coupon two columns wide by 2 inches deep. On the other side of that page, the advertiser buys that two columns by 2 inches directly behind the coupon and prints in this space copy similar to this:

Have you seen the coupon
On the other side of this page?

This procedure is practical only if the coupon is positioned properly within a standard-sized ad space.

What's in the Coupon? Put all the information that the reader needs in the coupon. Specifics build confidence on his part, and he should not feel that details have been left to chance. If the ad offers a choice of colors, sizes, or materials, include boxes for each possible choice the reader might want to make. This completeness of detail will increase response, for the reader will have the feeling that he can specify exactly what he wants without any chance of an error being made.

The company name and address should appear in the coupon. It also must appear outside the coupon as part of the other copy within the ad. Unless it appears in both locations, once the coupon has been clipped there is no name and address identification left in the ad.

Reader Service Cards

Reader service enables the reader of a publication to request information from a number of the advertisers in the publication simply by circling the appropriate numbers on the card, tearing it out, and sending it to the publication. Usually these cards (which are prepared by the publication, not by the advertisers) are bound into the publication but are perforated so that they can be torn out easily and are already printed with the publication's name and address and a postage permit. The mention of an ad on a reader service card can improve the pull even more; some advertisers have reported increases of 2,000 to 10,000 percent in inquiries made because of reader service cards.

While such cards do increase the pull of an ad tremendously, just as the coupon does, the ratio of inquiries to sales suffers far more than is true of the coupon. Not only are many requests for information sent simply because it is such an easy thing to do, but also lower-echelon personnel who have no purchasing power in an organization often will return the cards. Thus the cost of handling inquiries skyrockets, and the ratio of inquiries to sales is hurt.

Because of this, many publications now insist that anyone who uses his company's name when returning a reader service card identify his position with the company. This enables the advertiser to decide whether or not that particular inquiry is worth following up.

Publications make no charge for offering reader service cards to their advertisers, and those advertisers who want bulk inquiries can find a bonanza in the cards.

Mailing Lists

The sale of mailing lists is a big business today. Giant companies offer ZIP-coded lists (value: you actually can select neighborhoods) covering every possible breakdown of professional, economic, geographic, recreational, educational, and even sociopsychological interest. You can buy general or specialized lists of names, in any quantity (subject only to the maximum number of available names in that category) and in random or specific geographic areas. Prices usually range from $12 to $40 per thousand names, depending on the value and complexity of the list.

One recent list-availability mailing by a medium-sized list company carried such names as:

- 4,137 nurseries rated above $20,000 for $32 per 1,000 names

- 4,036 nonmetallic quarries and mines for $21 per 1,000 names

- 63,719 public elementary schools for $21 per 1,000 names

- 362 Mennonite churches, $20 for entire list

- 6,114 photography studios rated above $5,000 for $29 per 1,000 names

Inspecting available lists often gives you an idea that might not otherwise occur; it may open up a whole new speculative type of mailing. And all professional listing companies guarantee accuracy and delivery within 95 percent.

In addition to the standard gummed labels (with carbon copies at a nominal cost to use for follow-up mailings), list companies will supply the names on your own business envelopes, on index cards, on sheets of paper, and in some cases on punched cards or magnetic tape for computer use.

In a computerized age, choice of the geographic area and decisions concerning demographics (the "who") are equally important in list selection. The most frequently used specific or specialized lists are the subscription lists of community newspapers and of trade publications. The first pinpoints community-minded adults within a certain geographic area; the second pinpoints people within a specific industry or business.

If your customers mirror the readership of *Chain Store Age*, for instance, the publication's list is a good bet to use. The only problems with publication lists are that some publications refuse to sell their lists and that those that are available often are in the form of stamped or printed labels with many abbreviations that identify them as impersonal mass mailing.

On the local level, the telephone directory can produce both a general list and a number of specific lists. The White Pages are unselective in that they cross economic, ethnic, and professional boundaries. They are "mass" rather than selective—although some cities do have directories that list names and addresses by neighborhood, permitting more selection, since neighborhoods tend to have known characteristics. The Yellow Pages offer a no-cost source of industrial and commercial names within specific categories. These can be supplemented by such publications as *The Thomas Directory*, a nationwide listing of companies and their executives according to industrial classifications.

Source of Lists. Standard Rate and Data Service, Inc., has a semiannual book, *Direct Mail List Rates and Data.* This comprehensive volume carries sources of business lists, consumer lists, and farm lists, with every conceivable category from Protestant churchwomen's organizations (145,000 at $23 per thousand) to estate planning and trust lawyers (15,000 at $27.50 per thousand) to cattle ranchers (63,000 at $20 per thousand).[1]

If you know your market, obtain a list that mirrors that market. If you are trying to find your market, use a more general list and check the results carefully to find out where your market lies.

A Few Warnings. If you decide to compile your own list, remember that the U.S. Postal Service prohibits third class mailings that omit ZIP codes. Remember, too, that a list that comes to you for $30 per thousand on pressure-sensitive labels costs 3 cents per name, usually far less than your own cost of compilation.

However, be aware of the depersonalization process that is taking place in our society. A name that obviously has been machine-printed on a label is impersonal and runs a greater risk of rejection. Consider the value of typed or handwritten names as opposed to automated labels.

Postal Laws and Regulations

The U.S. Postal Service (as of publication date) recognizes four classes of mail outlined below. Changing regulations make it advisable to check with your local postmaster for the latest regulations.

> **First class mail:** local or out-of-town letters weighing 12 ounces or less; postcards; business-reply envelopes and cards; airmail letters, postcards, packages weighing 9 ounces or less.

[1] *Direct Mail List Rates and Data,* July, 1973.

Second class mail: periodicals and newspapers.

Third class mail: everything else—circulars, books, catalogs, printed matter, seeds and plants weighing less than 16 ounces. To qualify for third class bulk rate, mail must be ZIP-coded and must be comprised of at least 200 identical pieces or 50 pounds. Under certain circumstances, third class mail may be sealed.

Fourth class mail: parcel post.

The Mixed Blessing of First Class Mail.   First class mail costs more to send than third class mail. First class mail is also more effective than third class mail.

Since third class mail has last priority in handling—on some occasions being delivered so late that the "sale" or "order before expiration date" offer advertised in the mailing is outdated—the speed advantage of first class mail is obvious.

Psychologically, first class mail has a bigger advantage: the recipient is more likely to open it. Most individuals expect a first class letter to be personal. Obviously, third class mail is impersonal, because individual messages cannot qualify for third class rate.

But true mass mailings, those above 50,000 units, cannot logically be sent by first class mail. Costs simply spiral upward too rapidly.

Machine-stamped first class mail has little psychological benefit over third class. The first class benefit lies in the stamp itself, and a postage meter eliminates the personalization that the stamp represents.

Although first class postage is more expensive, the cost gap between first and third class has narrowed. Under some circumstances, first class mail may even be less expensive, for third class mail must be bundled according to destination and this can be a time-consuming business.

Considering all this, is first class mail always a better idea? The answer cannot be an absolute yes. However, generally first class mail pulls a response in excess of its advanced cost. In any specific situation where there are circumstances that might lessen the advantage, testing with half first class and half third class certainly would be in order.

Updating Lists.   Marking mail "Address Correction Requested" will keep lists current. For a fee of 10 cents per unit forwarded, the Postal Service will supply to the sender the new address and ZIP code.

Double postcards also are often valuable in updating mailing lists. Many users of direct mail initiate a campaign to inactive customers, sending them a double postcard that offers some incentive or premium for returning ZIP-code information on the reply card. Some mailers report better than 80 percent response to such mailings, which enables the mailing service to ZIP code the address and thereby make possible third class mailings.

Prestamped Reply Envelopes. In almost every case, it is a sadly wasteful technique to prestamp business-reply mail with a first class stamp. Business-reply envelopes or cards should simply bear the permit frank (easily obtained from any Postal Service branch), and then those envelopes and cards that are returned are delivered postage due at first class rates.

Look at the difference: A mailing of 10,000 pieces, each of which contains a reply envelope with a 10-cent stamp, has a reply-stamp-cost factor of $1,000, plus the cost of affixing the stamps, perhaps another $100. A 20 percent return means that 2,000 returns have cost $1,100 in postage. By printing the permit frank on the envelope, those 2,000 returns would have cost only $200 in postage.

The one exception to this rule seems to be in the case of fund-raising and nonprofit organizations, which regularly report that the use of pasted-on first class stamps on the reply envelopes enclosed with their letters soliciting contributions seems to increase response far in excess of the additional cost of the stamps. (But few marketers run nonprofit operations intentionally.) Colorful special-issue stamps are particularly effective.

Cost Control

With the possible exception of the largest, most knowledgeable direct mail advertisers, users could control costs far better than they do. Where is there fat to be trimmed? In addition to the tips about artwork and printing covered in Chapter 3, here are the most important areas to consider:

- Weight
- Size
- Paper

- Enclosures
- Number of pieces printed
- Checking results

Weight. Every day, advertising mailings cost their senders thousands of extra dollars because their weight, even a fraction of an ounce, edges the postage cost into a higher category. Before printing anything, assemble blank pieces of paper of the same proposed weight as the mailing itself. Include everything that will be included in the mailing: a piece of literature, a business-reply card or envelope, and so on. Then weigh it carefully.

In first class mail, the weight of each individual piece is the deciding factor. If you don't weigh your mailing unit first, you may complete all your printing and then discover that a quarter of an ounce per unit has doubled your mailing cost. In bulk third class mail, total weight is the determining factor—and even a quarter of an ounce can add up when multiplied in terms of large mailings.

However, do not assume that the lightest-weight mail is the best. Simply be aware of weight as a cost factor. It may be that a heavier paper is more impressive or is required for the type of printing planned.

Size. This point was discussed in Chapter 3. Most printing papers are produced in standard sizes. Examine the most common size, 17 by 22 inches. Any even division of this size enables you to use every scrap of paper. For example, from a 17 by 22 piece of paper you can cut four 8½ by 11 sheets; if you want a jumbo size, you can cut two 11 by 17 sheets. However, if you want a "custom" size, say a 9 by 12-inch sheet, you can cut only two such sheets, with a paper wastage of more than 40 percent. Thus your paper cost, based on that standard size, is no more for an 11 by 17 piece than it is for a 9 by 12-inch piece.

Adherence to standard uses of the 17 by 22 master sheet size represents an opportunity for the individual who can depart from standard cuts and folds and yet not waste paper. This can be done by planning several different pieces, printed together, using the entire sheet.

For example, one piece can be 11 by 14 inches. A second unit use can be three single folds, each 8½ by 5½. An unusual strip, folded several times in mailing, is 3 by 22. The remaining piece, 5½ by 2½, can be an enclosure, coupon, or envelope stuffer. See the illustration on the next page.

If the paper is grained, a consideration is the effect of pieces that should look the same but which run counter to each other in grain. If you plan carefully you will not have to use all the paper for the same mailing,

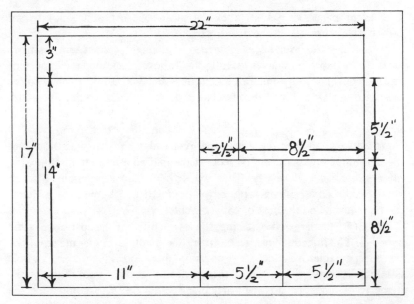

A 17- by 22-inch master sheet of paper may be divided in this way to enable the user of direct mail to depart from standard cuts and folds and yet not waste paper.

which will prevent a "one-paper" look that is boring and unemphatic. (Some office forms, the paper for which is of no consequence, can be included in figuring the use of leftover paper.)

One approach to figuring an appropriate size is to cut a newspaper sheet into a 17 by 22-inch size, and then experiment with cutting and folding it. It is possible to work out many variations in sizes without wasting paper.

And what about the envelope? Unless your mailing is of enormous volume, it probably is wasteful to use anything except the standard sizes of envelopes.

Paper Quality. Two pieces of paper that look almost identical may have a cost differential of 50 percent. This can be due to the actual cost of producing a particular paper, but it also can be due to the availability of that paper at a specific print shop. It always pays to ask the printer for samples of paper he has in stock, or available, just as it pays to get competitive estimates on the printing itself.

If you are a careful buyer of paper, you might collect samples from some of the paper companies listed in the Yellow Pages, along with current prices. You may find some price surprises—and you also may find colors and textures that will influence the entire design of your mailing.

Enclosures. Gathering the enclosures (collating) and stuffing them into the envelopes is expensive. The more items that go into each envelope, the more expensive collating is. Thus, when items can be combined, as an order blank and a business-reply envelope might be, the number of items can be reduced and the cost of collating cut.

However, the larger the mailing, the less significant the cost of collating becomes. The huge mailings sent out by the giant consumer magazines or the oil companies may include a dozen or more individual items—a whole evening's reading, if they get the attention of the recipient. Each of the items is designed to do one particular selling job, thus eliminating the confusion that can result from a multiplicity of offers on a single sheet.

Number of Pieces Printed. Analyze the costs involved in the typical printed piece. They include:

- Writing
- Layout
- Typesetting
- Art and/or photos
- Pasteup

- Plates or printing negatives
- Makeready
- Paper
- Printing

Of this group of nine elements of cost, only the last two—paper and printing—are variables. If you were to plan a printed piece with a press run of 1,000 or 1,000,000, the cost of the first seven elements would be identical. However, the cost per unit printed would drop as the volume or length of the run was increased.

For instance, suppose those fixed costs totaled $600. If you print 1,000 units, your cost per unit, excluding paper and printing, would be 60 cents—which obviously is prohibitive, even though the individual fixed costs themselves are modest. However, if you print 10,000 units, the cost per unit, excluding paper and printing, drops to 6 cents, a more reasonable figure.

However, if you work with relatively small mailing lists how can you take advantage of this? Here are some possibilities:

- You can quantity-run one color that has nonchanging elements. For example, your address, your logo, and perhaps your heading (as in a newsletter) do not change often. Other elements, deliberately reused, also can help you create an individual image. Pick a color for these, and run a full year's worth on standard paper. Then, each month or whenever needed, use this preprinted supply as stock to prepare your regular mailings. Savings will be substantial.

- Increase the size of your list. If you can reach an additional 2,000 prospects for a fraction of the cost of your basic list, it may pay to experiment with peripheral and speculative lists.

- Why not try to sell your mailing piece to another company in your field, one that is not competitive? For example, if you are a retailer handling a fairly common assortment of goods, you can offer your materials to anyone in the same business located well outside your own market area. The result of a mailing with samples and a note saying, "This is yours exclusively in your market for $100," may be a pleasant surprise. And when someone wants to use those materials, you can add to the length of your run, thus saving money while making money (the printer simply switches company logos and addresses at the proper points in the run, a relatively quick and inexpensive process).

Checking Results

"How'd your mailing pull?" "I don't know—pretty good, I guess. . ." That second speaker is the same marketer who knows to a unit exactly how much inventory he carries and how many 8-ounce bottles of a particular product he ordered three years ago. Yet the best way to control costs is to use the more effective types of mailings—and the only way to know which mailings pull the best results is to measure those results scientifically.

Note the use of that word "scientifically." An "eyeball check" is not sufficient. A guess is not good enough. This measurement has to be accurate and exact. There are times when a 2-inch stack of returns looks big, and there are times when exactly the same number of returns looks insignificant.

The best way to check results is often impossible for the smaller marketer: a split-run. Split-runs are mailings of different types which offer the same product or service at the same price and are sent to similar lists.

For example, a marketer might try a split-run mailing of 10,000 pieces. Of these pieces 5,000 would be colorful brochures, heavily illustrated, mailed to the first half of a list (perhaps alphabetically divided, mailed to A through M). The other 5,000 pieces would be a simple, mimeographed, no-nonsense announcement of product and price, with an order blank.

Another split-run mailing might be identical in every detail except for the covering letter. Half the pieces would contain a warm, friendly, and humorous letter. The other half of the pieces would have a factual, explicit, and impersonal letter.

In both cases, the final job would be to check to see which type of mailing produced the most replies. (Rather than dividing a list alphabetically, an even better way is to use two different colors for order envelopes, sending one color to one half the list and the other color to the other half of the list. The colors could be mixed together before collating, and thus their distribution would be random rather than alphabetical. A simple visual check of the envelopes as the orders are received will tell you at a glance which mailing produced best.)

Test-mailing a list also is important. Businesses dealing in cost per lead or cost per order know the importance of testing the lists they use. In selling smokers' pipes by mail, which group would order the most: school teachers, heads of companies, or people who have ordered sporting goods by mail? The answer: Who knows?

Therefore, if you plan to buy many thousands of names from a mailing service and have no previous knowledge of that market, it is wise to test that list first. When results start to come in, get them both geographically and by any other criteria available. What you want to find out is:

- Who orders?
- At what time?
- From where?
- In what quantity?
- As a result of what mailing?

However, always beware of overchecking. You are in the research business only to the extent that the results of that research can be put to practical and usually immediate use. It is too easy to fall into the time-wasting pattern of cross-checking results so carefully and so laboriously that neither you nor anyone else ever can use the information you learn.

Knowledge about your market and knowledge about your skill in producing effective direct mail campaigns should be the goals of any checking you do. Here are some common goals:

- Where is your market?
- What is your market?
- Who is your market?
- What appeal is most effective in reaching your market?
- How much response has this mailing pulled?
- How can the next mailing be designed to pull even more?

RADIO

Once radio was primarily a medium for delivering sales messages to people at home—from an advertiser's point of view. Today, radio counts people on the go an important part of its audience. Few cars today are minus a radio, and we have become a nation that spends considerable time on wheels. Transistor radios go to the ball park, the beach, the picnic table, and even provide music and news as people walk down the street.

Radio advertising slumped in the 1950s, but now it is strong and growing again, thanks not only to the increased mobility of radios but also to the way programming has changed to meet today's changed culture. The emphasis used to be on soap operas during the day and formal half-hour or hour programs in the evening, but today's stations are likely to concentrate on music or news or conversation or special ethnic interests, and the mood is usually strictly informal.

Radio advertising has changed to match the new slant in programming. National advertisers used to put the larger part of their advertising money for radio into full or partial sponsorship of a specific program. Today, the standby of the local advertiser, spot advertising, the 1-minute, 30-second, or even briefer commercial, is the most popular.

To make radio advertising pay off, a businessman has to choose the right station, the right time, and the right approach.

The Right Station

Most marketers operate in areas served by a number of radio stations. These range from clear-channel stations with programs heard throughout the country to local stations with a broadcast range limited to 30 or 50 miles. In general, stations can be divided according to the "circulation," the makeup of that circulation, and the prices charged and services offered.

Picking the right station is somewhat like picking the right newspaper or the right list to which you send a mailing. Know your market and then pick the station that caters to that market.

Circulation. The number of people who listen to a particular station are that station's circulation. This is a figure on which the station's advertising department usually has done research and about which they are delighted to explain, although sometimes somewhat less biased accounts are available from the various rating services. Circulation is based on the power of the station's transmitter, the areas in which reception is clear, the number of radio sets within those areas, and the number of those sets that are usually tuned to that station when they are turned on.

The power of the transmitter determines how far the sound that it sends will travel. However, within that radius there may be natural or man-made barriers that make reception indistinct in certain areas. Another problem is caused by stations of different strengths located close to each other on the radio band: the stronger station sometimes can overpower the sound of the weaker station, particularly in AM reception.

While the number of radio sets within the areas of clear reception is fairly easy to determine, finding out how many of them can be counted in the station's circulation obviously is more difficult. This requires using some method of audience measurement, a job handled with even reasonable efficiency only by trained researchers. However, the station itself usually will have the work of some research organization to back up its circulation figures.

Makeup of Circulation. Knowing that a station does a good job of reaching a specific number of people within a specific area is interesting—but it is useful only if the people who listen to the station qualify as your customers. Here, again, research done by or sponsored by the station probably will give you an answer. Stations usually have statistics that break down their circulations by age, sex, location, and often by race, ethnic group, and even special interests.

The programming itself is a good indication of the kind of people who listen, particularly today when so many stations concentrate on beaming their programming at specific target groups of people. There are stations that concentrate on news, others that concentrate on music, and others that concentrate on comment. There are those that talk in national terms and those that cover strictly local topics. There are stations that program for blacks, teen-agers, foreign-language groups, or even that group perhaps hardest to pinpoint, the middle-aged and middle class.

A small marketer of teen-age fashions might well do best to ignore the larger stations in his area and concentrate on whatever local station delivers the music and local news likely to be listened to by teen-agers. Such a station's audience obviously would be an ideal match for the marketer's target group of customers.

Prices and Services. Rates for commercial time on radio vary tremendously from station to station and according to the time of day the commercial is to be used.

The rate usually is based on the number of people listening to the station—and who they are. Normally those stations reaching the most people will have the highest rates. Each station has a rate card with a schedule of rates according to the time of day the commercial is to be used, with higher rates for peak listening hours and surcharges for special programs, and discounts according to the total number of commercials bought. From 6 a.m. to 9 a.m. and 4 p.m. to 7 p.m. are the peak listening hours for radio, the hours when more people listen to radio than watch television. During the evening, however, the television sets go on and rates for radio commercials drop sharply.

Most stations have some sort of advertising department that can help the marketer prepare his commercials, and some stations offer assistance in every phase of the job, from preparing the original script through broadcasting or recording the finished product.

Your own experience in writing or producing radio commercials will determine how useful such services are to you. If this is a new field for you, the availability of good professional help from a particular station, so long as that station's audience matches your market, is worth money to you.

The Right Time

We already have learned that the time of day plays a profound role in the structuring of radio stations' rate cards. To recapitulate: for most stations, morning drive time, 6 a.m. to 9 a.m., is most expensive; evening drive time, 4 p.m. to 7 p.m., is next most expensive.

The most expensive time may not produce the most business for you. It depends on what you have to sell. Selective buyers will adhere to the basic rule of profitable advertising outlined in Chapter 1: The most effective advertising is that which reaches, at the lowest possible cost, the most people who can and will buy what you have to sell. The rule is easy to apply in radio, where audiences are specific.

A supermarket chain, for instance, knows that housewives tend to do their major food shopping on Fridays, with much of it spilling over into Saturday. Therefore, spots around housewife-oriented programs Thursday and Friday probably would get the largest audience. That marketer of teen fashions, however, might choose to use disc jockey shows, running his commercials from midafternoon through the evening weekdays, and all day Saturdays and Sundays, because stations catering to teen-agers retain their audiences during the evening hours.

SECTION I

RATE CARD # 29

AM ONLY

WPAT

Rate Card

EFFECTIVE 9/3/73

	5X	10X	15X
5:30–10AM MON–SAT	90	85	80
10AM–2:50PM MON–FRI	90	85	80
2:50PM–7:55PM MON–FRI	95	90	85
7:55PM–1AM MON–SUN	80	75	70
10AM–8PM SAT & SUN	85 (80 FM)	80 (75 FM)	75 (70 FM)

ALL RATES ARE FOR 1 MINUTE ANNOUNCEMENTS

30 SECOND ANNOUNCEMENTS 80% OF MINUTE RATE

10 SECOND ANNOUNCEMENTS 80% OF MINUTE RATE
NON–PRE–EMPTIBLE

10 SECOND ANNOUNCEMENTS 60% OF MINUTE RATE
PRE–EMPTIBLE

1396 Broad Street, Clifton, N. J. 07013
(201) 472-0930   (212) 688-9300
A Capital Cities Station

Courtesy of WPAT, Clifton, N.J.

Each radio station has a rate card showing how rates vary according to the time of day the commercial is to be aired.

The Right Approach

Few advertisers buy full sponsorship of radio programs today, although this was a popular method of advertising a few decades ago. Instead, advertisers choose between buying segments of programs and buying spots. This, in contrast to full sponsorship of a program, is usually called "participation advertising," in that several advertisers "participate" in sponsoring a program.

Commercials may be presented live or they may be recorded. In either case, a script must be prepared. The only exception is the occasional radio personality who prefers to deliver commercials on his program based on a fact sheet rather than a script.

Segment Buying. When a marketer sponsors a program segment, he buys 5, 10, 15, or perhaps 30 minutes of a specific radio program. During that time, the only commercials the station broadcasts are that advertiser's. This is the same technique used when an advertiser sponsors an entire program.

Segment buying has its best impact when a marketer uses it on a regular basis. Buying a segment only occasionally has none of the impact of having the commercials run on a specific program at a specific time day after day or week after week. It is another illustration of synergism: repeated advertising has a cumulative impact greater than the sum of the individual commercials. "And now, the weather report, brought to you by..." broadcast at the same time day after day firmly fixes both the marketer's name and his products in the minds of the listeners.

Popular time slots for segment advertising are on disc jockey shows, news programs, sports programs, weather reports, and traffic reports. Even the time signal can be an effective segment to buy.

Spots. The amount spent on radio spot commercials is far larger than that spent for segment buying. Usually, spots are 60, 30, or 10 seconds long. Seven-word "reminder spots" are growing in popularity. On most stations, spots may be purchased on a "fixed position" basis, in which the advertiser is assured of broadcast at a specific time, or on a "run of station" basis, in which the station, in exchange for a lower rate, broadcasts commercials as it wishes, during the entire broadcast day. Midway between these two procedures is the preemptible spot, which is bought conditionally, at a low rate: if the station finds a buyer at full rate, the preemptible spot is not run.

Spots naturally cost considerably less than segments. However, do not assume that buying a 5-minute segment of a program will result in a 5-minute commercial. Typically, the sponsor of such a segment can anticipate opening and closing mentions, plus one 30-second or 1-minute commercial. In some cases the cost of spots is so close to the cost of short program sponsorship that little dollar difference exists.

Live or Recorded? Radio commercials may be delivered live, may be recorded, or may be a combination of the two—but the type of program in which the commercial is to be used often determines how that commercial is to be presented. Live commercials, read by the announcer or emcee of a particular show, are popular if the show is run by a name personality. When the disc jockey who is the idol of the teen-agers reads a commercial about the place to buy clothes, that youth audience remembers. Individual stations might require that a commercial inserted in a news program be recorded, so that there is a clear distinction between the reporting of the news and the delivery of the commercial.

Live commercials, therefore, are particularly desirable if they are read by someone important to the listeners. Recorded commercials, on the other hand, can guarantee the advertiser a consistently perfect presentation of his message and can allow him to use music and complex sound effects. Musical jingles are always recorded; some jingles have a musical "bridge" during which the local announcer cuts in with local or timely copy.

A station can offer the advertiser recorded background sounds to increase the appeal of a live message. The recording might be of a cash register ringing, a plane taking off, a doorbell ringing, a circus band, a crowd of people—whatever fits into the script and adds another dimension to the sound of the announcer's voice reading the words of the script. A number of sound effects are available, on LP discs, for purchase. Copyright laws make it unwise to use recorded music without making an arrangement with the copyright owner. (A copyright is valid for 28 years and may be renewed for an additional 28 years.)

The Message to Get Across

There are three important points to remember in creating a script for a radio commercial. They involve merchandise, price, and continuity. Regardless of the kind of product you want to sell and regardless of the way you think you can sell it, these points are pertinent. Cleverness is helpful but is no substitute for merchandise or price.

Merchandise. Almost any consumer want, from product through image, can be sold by radio advertising. You can convince people to take advantage of a special sale on ski boots next week, or you can convince them that you are the first store they should try when they want gardening supplies, insurance, or, for that matter, advertising.

However, merchandise advertised via radio must be described by words alone. In all other media, some form of illustration can be used, if necessary. There is no way of using an illustration in a radio commercial—except the picture that the announcer can paint with words. And there is a genuine possibility for advantage in this appeal to the listener's imagination: this is one reason why radio can be such a useful image-builder for a marketer.

Often, the visualization of an item or a service which is generated in the radio listener's mind is even more favorable to that item or product than would occur were a visual presentation to be made. The listener's imagination is brought into play, and the image-building possibilities are enhanced.

Price. Radio is not usually regarded as a prime medium for products in which multiple prices must be mentioned. This is because broadcast advertising lacks the benefit of referral: the newspaper reader can clip the ad and refer back to the price; the radio listener must depend on his memory.

Therefore, if the commercial requires price information, that information must be emphasized and repeated if possible. It is a misuse of radio as an advertising medium to write commercials that include lists of grocery prices that the listener will not remember.

Continuity. The word "continuity" has various meanings. In radio advertising, the term is used to refer to any copy that is read on the air.

Writing good radio continuity is like writing any other piece of selling copy. It should include all the pertinent points; it should be prepared with the benefit to the customer in mind; it should be clearly and succinctly worded. Just as in writing direct mail copy, there is no place for grandiose or tricky wording, because the listener has no way to refer back to words that may have slipped past him. Clarity is even more important in radio copy, for a radio listener cannot ask the station to repeat something he didn't understand.

Thus radio continuity can afford to be somewhat more repetitive than other forms of selling messages. The target individual receives the message only as sound. There is no picture to look at, no photograph or illustration that can be referred to. The points must be clear, distinct, and easy to remember. This is one reason for the success of the radio jingle, which combines product identification with a message easy to remember.

More than in any other medium, the inexperienced writer has an opportunity to try to be clever in radio commercials. Were he to try his hand at humor writing in television, the chances of his work hitting the airwaves would be less, since the cost of producing television commercials prohibits casual production.

During much of the 1960s and early 1970s, one school of advertising writing rejected as stuffy, old-fashioned, and square any commercial that relied on straightforward selling copy. The result was a confusion of commercials that often entertained without selling. Since any medium as quickly contagious as radio results in almost instant imitation of any procedure, much of what was created, especially on the local level, had little sales value.

The test of a radio commercial's validity is whether, hearing the commercial, the typical listener is favorably impressed not by the writer's cleverness but by the product. Cleverness works but only if tied to selling principles. A warning: In this age of skepticism, attempts to be clever may well be a liability rather than an asset.

TELEVISION

Considering today's marketplace, the marketer who asks what value motion pictures can have for him is naive. A motion picture can help him show his product line to best advantage; a motion picture can help his salesmen describe his plant; a motion picture can illustrate the benefits of doing business with him; a motion picture can show his product in use or his service in action; a motion picture can be a tireless, entertaining salesman whose sales talk never falters.

Perhaps most intriguing in today's television-oriented world, a motion picture can be a marketer's tool for reaching that tremendous television audience. A motion picture, in the form of a television commercial, can put his advertising in one of today's major media.

Television is not a medium reserved for the giants in marketing. It can be, and gradually is becoming, an important sales promotion weapon for marketers of all sizes. Handling this weapon efficiently and yet economically requires an understanding of television's technicalities, the kinds of costs involved, and what you can and cannot handle by doing it yourself.

Technicalities

A live-action commercial often is shot in 60-, 30-, 20-, and 10-second versions, because the additional cost of having the different lengths is nominal. The set and the message remain the same; the wording and the action may be condensed but not made appreciably different. Often shorter versions of a commercial are made from the "outs"—takes that have not been used for the longer version.

There are three standard gauges of motion picture film:

- 35mm, which is restricted in use largely to motion picture theatres.

- 16mm, which has limited theatrical use but is the standard gauge for television and also has wide use in classrooms, businesses, and homes.

- 8mm, which has widespread use in home movies and astonishing growth in business use.

In today's market, most filmed television commercials are in 16mm gauge. Some are filmed in 35mm and then reduced to 16mm, especially if the possibility exists that the same footage may be incorporated into a theatrical trailer.

Sound film runs at 24 frames per second. This means that there are 1,440 separate pictures each minute. In 16mm, with 40 frames to the foot, there are 36 feet of film for each minute. Thus a 10-minute film is 360 feet long, plus the usual head and tail thread-up leaders.

Many newsreel producers shoot their film "single system"—that is, with the sound recorded directly onto the film. But the demands of quality dictate that commercials be shot "double system," with sound recorded originally on magnetic tape and later transferred to the 16mm gauge as part of the editing process.

Costs[2]

In low-budget shops, a live-action, 1-minute color commercial will average from $500 to $2,000 to produce. Some commercials have cost $40,000 and more, but these are heavily produced commercials that have included, for example, fleets of automobiles in strange or exotic settings. One commercial, featuring many dancing girls and a soup can rising from the stage, was reported to cost $154,000.

Animated cartoons are popular for commercials, both because they appeal to all age ranges and because their message may be symbolic rather than actual and yet be understood easily. An animated commercial usually will cost from $7,000 to $12,000 per one-minute spot, a cost that becomes more significant when one realizes that, because of their novelty value, such commercials tend to "wear out" faster.

Many commercials combine live action with animation to combine reality with entertainment. Such spots usually open with an animated sequence to get attention and then use a live action scene to show and sell the product.

Do-It-Yourself Possibilities

Most major manufacturers of consumer products make available film or videotape commercials for local use by their local dealers. These usually are referred to as open-end dealer spots: the commercials do not run full length; instead, they are several seconds short so that the local dealer can insert his name, usually on a slide, to complete and personalize the commercial.

However, you can make your own commercials—with a little skill and sometimes with a little outside help. Any marketer with a good sales promotion staff, or with access to a good sales promotion staff, already

[2] The figures given in this section are derived from the author's personal experience.

has much of the talent he needs. What specialized technical skills or creative talents he does not have, he can buy from the outside as needed for a particular job.

The Script. If the marketer's own sales promotion staff handles the preparation of the script, the copywriter may well be someone more used to printed media copy than to writing for television. The difference is a matter of technique of presentation, not of choice of selling points or of the importance of emphasizing customer benefits. That copywriter first should prepare a draft of the kind of copy that could be used to sell a specific product in a printed medium and then rework copy into a visual sell to match the visual medium.

This assures that his copy will include a major selling point and amplification of that point, covered from the customer's point of view, written in a "talking" rather than "writing" style.

The key to a good television script is that it creates a personal contact with the television viewer. The commercial actually reaches out of the set and speaks to the viewer, just as a salesperson does when a customer is across the counter. That sense of direct contact, of immediacy, is what keeps the viewer looking at his set during the commercial instead of letting his attention drift.

Usually the writer indicates the kind of pictures or action that should accompany the text. Figuring out exactly what props and action should be used may be someone else's job (a store with a good display staff has a rich source of talent for setting a stage), but the writer outlines the visual presentation. The words and the action should be intermeshed to be effective.

Always make sure the name of your company or brand, whichever is more important, is prominently featured in the commercial. A store will emphasize its name (and perhaps its location and the hours that it is open). A manufacturer may want to emphasize the brand name of the product being offered and perhaps include a list of places where it can be purchased. Repeated name identification costs nothing extra and may well be the most effective commercial for the typical low-budget advertiser.

Filming. Can you shoot your own filmed television commercial? Theoretically, yes. Any 16mm camera is capable of shooting acceptable footage.

Local sound laboratories, editing services, or film laboratories can handle adding the sound track to the film.

First, remember that all professional color film is balanced for 3,200 degrees on the Kelvin color temperature scale. This means that exterior scenes shot with professional color film require a filter to prevent a too-blue effect, since daylight registers about 5,600 degrees on the Kelvin scale. If you want to shoot interior scenes, such as the inside of your store or warehouse, check color temperature as well as the amount of light, for different kinds of lighting have different Kelvin readings.

Increased use of color film has made it almost as economical as black-and-white. At this writing, the most commonly used 16mm stock is either Eastman #7247 negative color or Eastman #7252 Commercial Ektachrome, both of which are designed for printing rather than for projection of the original. If a sound track is to be added and prints are to be made, avoid home movie film; this film is not designed for printing, and color densities will be affected adversely.

Generally, 8mm film is not accepted, nor do television stations usually have the equipment to project it. True, 8mm prints are considerably less expensive than 16mm prints. Therefore, if you want to make multiple prints from your original commercial (for example, a print of the film for each of ten salesmen or each of a dozen or more stores or exhibits), the best way may be to shoot the film in 16mm and then either print by reduction or make a "dupe negative" for multiple-print production at low cost.

(If you are planning to make multiple copies for use by salesmen or in exhibits, make sure the prints are matched to the projectors. If the projectors are conventional reel types, have the prints mounted on reels; if they are automatic or cartridge types, order the prints in the proper mount or cartridge. And whenever possible, instruct the laboratory to treat the prints with a chemical hardener; at a cost of a fraction of a cent per foot, this adds considerable longevity to print life.)

Sound. When working out the narration, remember that the mechanics of film dictate a policy adopted by most television stations of requiring that the first 1½ seconds have unmodulated sound track—that is, that the sound for the commercial does not begin until the picture has run for 1½ seconds. The sound track, therefore, is always shorter than the picture, and writing a commercial that is overly wordy will result in a spot that either runs too long and requires cutting or necessitates too rapid narration in order to include all the words.

Unless your voice is unusually good, do not be the announcer for your commercial. It is better to have a silent film with narration by the announcer in the sound booth at the television station than to have an unprofessional sound track. Yes, the informal touch can be effective, particularly if a local retailer, for instance, films shots of his own displays to show what he is selling and uses his own salespeople as his actors. However, informality succeeds only when it is professionally, deftly done. Poorly handled informality simply appears awkward and clumsy—impressions that do not make a sale.

Some businessmen carry their do-it-yourself filmmaking only through the photography, which is the most expensive part to buy outside, and then turn over the film to a professional for editing and sound matching.

Companies capable of handling any film work needed are listed in the Yellow Pages under the categories "Motion Picture Producers" and "Motion Picture Laboratories." Always get competitive prices, regardless of the job you want done. There often is a wide variance among producers and laboratories.

Videotape. For the local television advertiser, videotape often can offer the solution to low-cost production of totally acceptable quality. It is possible to produce three or four videotape commercials at a price comparable to a single film commercial. Most stations will negotiate for the use of their videotape equipment and crews by the hour. (Home videotape recorders are not standard TV size.)

The limitation of videotape is its lack of portable equipment. Only professional videotape studios in the major production centers such as New York and Los Angeles have hand-held color cameras that afford total portability. Since few local stations are likely to have this equipment available, all shooting must be done in the studio, none on location.

The most important point for the local advertiser to remember is that he must arrive for the taping session completely ready to start shooting. If the product or container looks bad or shoddy, if the commercials run too long, if backgrounds have not been worked out, if sequences cannot be run directly after each other and subsequent tape editing is required, the cost will rise sharply.

Selecting the Time

You have a filmed commercial. How are you going to use it? Rates for television time vary in the same way that rates for radio time vary. Those times at which the largest number of people are watching their television sets and those programs with the biggest audience command the highest rates.

Most television stations have time classifications for various periods of the day and night, with rates to match those classifications. For example, at one televison station class "AAA" time may be the prime evening hours; "AA" time is the hour or 90 minutes adjacent to the prime hours; "A" time is the next most heavily watched period; "B" time represents the daytime hours; and "C" time is late at night and early in the morning. Some stations have separate rates for weekend programming and for "specials."

Currently, the 30-second commercial is the most popular length; depending on the station, a 30-second commercial costs anywhere from 50 to 70 percent as much as a 60-second commercial. Its popularity is based on the theory that the relative impact is greater than the difference in cost. By 1972, according to the Television Bureau of Advertising, 74 percent of the $1.4 billion spent on TV spot broadcasts went into 30-second spots.

As he does with all other media, a marketer choosing the time to schedule his television commercials should choose that time when he is likely to reach the largest number of people who can and will buy what he has to sell. Smaller marketers, therefore, and retailers in particular, often can take advantage of less expensive time on the local television station. Many such retailers aim much of their sales promotion at women, and often the largest audience of women can be reached by using a daytime commercial.

And the Campaign

Some marketers use television only on special occasions, as an extra push behind Christmas selling, for instance, or for Easter fashions, or as a back-to-school promotion. In some cases, the television campaign may use a saturation technique: within a single week or two, the company uses everything from short identifications to minutes to put its message in front of the television audience. (A few stations offer 2-minute spots: the rate is twice that of a 1-minute spot.)

Other marketers, however, use television as a regular part of the sales promotion program, using commercials throughout the year that carefully project the same theme and image while promoting different products. Usually such a campaign is based on buying spots on a regular schedule.

It is up to you to decide how you can use television. Except for direct mail, it is the most expensive medium per person reached; but it is by far the most effective medium available today, and properly used it can be stunningly effective.

NOW, APPLY WHAT YOU'VE LEARNED

Test your ability to design and execute a direct mail campaign and to use broadcast media, based on the information in this chapter.

1. Collect your business mail for one week. Then select the sales letter, addressed to you, that you regard as the dullest of the lot. Rewrite the letter and send it to the original writer as a suggested replacement. (You won't offend unless your accompanying letter is unpleasant.)

2. Using this same collection of mail you've received, separate those mailings in which the envelopes are blank except for the printed name and address. Using the sales literature as a key, experiment with writing or printing on the face of the envelope to add some selling power.

3. Deliberately write a bad sales letter to a typical customer or client: overlong first sentence, clichés, generalized nonaction words. Outdo yourself to make the letter dull. Then rewrite the letter and make it sparkle, using the rules outlined in this chapter.

4. Write the same sales letter three different ways. Don't just substitute words; use three totally different ideas. Then make up a customer or client list, and, from your knowledge of the individuals, decide which of the three sales letters would appeal best to each individual on the list; in doing so, put in

writing the reason why, and you'll have the key to successful future mailings.

5. You manufacture an artificial sweetener sold in bulk only to hotels, restaurants, and institutions. Plan the components of a direct mailing to present your product to the proper buyers.

6. Add one color to each of the component parts of the mailing planned for activity 5, and justify the use of that color. Then plan a piece of literature in which the paper is a color other than white, the ink a color other than black.

7. From a mailing list company, select five separate lists of buyers for prefabricated sauna baths to whom you might send a mailing. Explain the reason for choosing each list.

8. You operate a chain of six dry-cleaning stores. Using all available information from two local radio stations, write an evaluation that indicates which station you would use and why.

9. Using the rate card and all available information from a local television station, plan to spend $10,000 in spot broadcasting over a one-month period. Explain how the money would be spent. (Assume that you operate the chain of dry-cleaning stores mentioned above.)

10. Plan a filmed television commercial for your chain of dry-cleaning stores. Explain how, without requiring professional studio assistance for the shooting itself, you would show your service to best and most visual advantage.

CHAPTER FIVE

Sales Promotion Methods

Some businessmen think of marketing only in terms of advertising; both their budgets and their attitudes reflect this error. Advertising, even spread over several types of media, is only one way of reaching customers. A multifaceted promotion program is far more likely to give a marketer the best return for his money.

Publicity is one of the major facets of a good sales promotion program. Publicity is sometimes thought of as free advertising—but a promotional investment may be required if publicity is to be effective and continuing. Building and running a good publicity program takes careful planning and enough budget to put those plans into the kind of action that wins a spotlight for the company or its products.

Public relations is a sales promotion method of growing concern to businessmen concerned with their image. Contrary to the belief of those who regard the words "public relations" and "publicity" as synonymous, they are not the same. *Publicity* is free advertising that a company obtains by sending out prepared information about its activities to a newspaper, magazine, or television or radio station for reporting. It is a part of the total public relations effort, but true public relations gives direction to the entire image-building concept. The growth of public relations as a profession is a testament to the growing need for communication among the businessman, his customers, and his own family of workers. Most marketers have developed a pattern of timing for promotions—but sometimes that pattern should be reexamined. For instance, almost every retailer puts on a promotional campaign before Christmas; many depend on this season alone to bring them half of their total annual sales. But sometimes other natural holiday tie-ins, such as Valentine's Day or Secretaries' Day, both promotional days frankly designed for commercial purposes, are ignored.

Current events are also good handles on which to hang promotions. Marketers have started using astronaut themes for both decorating and advertising whenever a new moon shot or planetary launch is underway or just completed. The success of a local sports team can be tied to specials and sales. "Election Bet Specials," "First Snowfall Specials," and "Spring Blossoms of Values" can, if timed properly and tied to in-store display, be clever and productive.

What may be a standard type of promotion for a retailer can be unique for a manufacturer or wholesaler. The businessman who sends personalized greetings at Thanksgiving may be sending the only greeting of this type that his customers receive.

A Warning. Although alertness to current events can help build a promotional theme, tie those promotions only to those events that have a positive, happy flavor. A "Pearl Harbor Day Sale" simply is in bad taste. Paradoxically, some negative business situations can spur one-shot sales boasts: "Going Out of Business Sales" and "Fire Sales" spell good fortune for the buyer through the obvious ill-fortune of the seller.

Most marketers also have determined which elements of the promotional mix are best suited to their businesses and the particular goals of a campaign. These elements may include publicity, public relations, display, exhibits, and audiovisual aids as well as any other activity designed to impart information that will aid in the sale of a product.

Display is a facet of sales promotion important to retailers. Promotion-minded retailers consider designing and setting up appropriate displays as important as keeping their stores properly stocked with merchandise. Window displays stop passersby and bring them into the store. Interior displays guide those customers through the store and do an important silent selling job right at the point of purchase.

Exhibits are a specialized form of display, used primarily by manufacturers and wholesalers (although sometimes by retailers) to display their wares at trade shows and conventions. Within an absolutely limited number of square feet, a good exhibit contains all the elements to catch the attention of visitors to the show and to help salesmen explain and discuss the company's products or services. Many modern exhibits are automated: they require no salesman to be present but function on their own, once set up.

Audiovisual aids are an exciting and rapidly growing field of sales promotion tools. Salesmen can carry a projector on sales calls. Films and tapes can be used effectively in exhibits and in store windows and interior displays to catch and hold the customer's interest and help do the selling job. A motion picture, even shown on a countertop screen, demands the attention of the passerby.

Even the telephone, ordinary and unimaginative as it may seem compared with some of the electronic audiovisual aids, is a potent sales promotion tool. People may skip over the ads; they may ignore the commercials; they may not look at the displays—but very few people can resist answering the ring of a telephone.

PUBLICITY

If you have a news item about your company or one of its products, any of the mass news media—newspapers, magazines, radio and television stations—may be interested in using it. And if one or more of the media do use the item, the result is valuable publicity for your company and its products. Such publicity seldom just happens; in a successful marketing operation, it is planned.

Sometimes the news does just happen: a new product is introduced; an important management change is made in the company. This is the kind of news that the publicity staff likes, because it consists of obvious, newsworthy occurrences. But even when such activities are not taking place, an alert publicity staff hunts for news to publicize—and usually finds some.

Influenced by high-powered fictional representations of publicity men shown in movies and books, a businessman may think only in terms of what is, for him, an impossible approach: the major planned "stunt" that may cost thousands of dollars. And, by limiting his thinking to these avenues, he overlooks what may be, for him, an even more effective use of publicity: a professional, straightforward news release to the trade publication serving his industrial or commercial potential customers or to the community newspaper serving a readership group whose specific geographic location is more valuable to him than would be the worldwide circulation of a publication that might be more glamorous but which his limited publicity budget could not hope to reach.

A vital point, other than that the information be favorable, is that the news really be newsworthy. A company that earns a reputation of releasing only real news and useful information will find that much of its publicity finds its way into the news media. The media will come to trust that company's offerings. A company that sends out promotional fluff instead of news, a company that swamps the media with releases in hopes that some of them will be used, will find that even its real news is greeted dubiously by the news media.

Here are examples of first sentences of news stories that belong in the media, the circulation of which includes important chunks of the company's customers (and therefore, the media in which the company is likely to be advertising):

- *Scarlet is the IN color this fall, if new fashions on display in the big downtown windows of the Smith Company are any criterion. . .*

- *A new method of writing auto insurance which will save the average motorist as much as $30 each year has been announced by the Patello Insurance Agency. . .*

- *"A bright red bathtub? It's the latest," says John Markhoff, head of Markhoff Plumbing Fixtures, which just received this area's first shipment of the newest look in bathtubs. . .*

- *The Malkin Hardware Company will be open from 9 a.m. until 9 p.m., Thanksgiving to Christmas. According to Tom Malkin, president of the store, the longer hours are intended to make it possible for those who work during the day to enjoy unhurried gift shopping during the evenings. . .*

On the trade and industrial level, news stories sometimes are even easier to find. If nothing whatever seems new and there are no new executive personnel or promotions to publicize, the same ingenuity that marks the entrepreneur in other aspects of business should apply here: Issue a comment on business conditions:

- *A definite upward trend in the sales of used cars in the under-21 market has been noted at MG Motor Company. . .*

- *New taxes have had "no effect whatever" on advertising specialty sales, according to a leading local supplier. . .*

- *"The BRIGHT LOOK has spurred sales of lighting fixtures," says the head of a large local electrical wholesale company. . .*

How to Prepare a News Release

The basic tool for transmitting publicity information to the news media is the news release. A simple test can tell you quickly whether your news release is professional: Read a news story in the newspaper or magazine to which the article is being sent; if yours has the same flavor and newsiness, it is professionally handled.

Note that the term no longer is "press release"; it is "news release." The emphasis is on "news." Here is a first sentence that does not succeed—because the story is not news; it is an undisguised piece of advertising, and no matter how it is set up it cannot be transformed miraculously into news:

John H. Cronquist, well-known local furrier, this week unveiled his stunning new collection of beautiful furs. Among the magnificent coats are an exquisite Autumn Haze mink, priced at $4,500. . .

Adjectives such as "stunning," "beautiful," "magnificent," and "exquisite" are advertising words, not news words. Merely leaving them out of the story doubles its chances of publication. The rule: Write news, not puff. Would a staff reporter hand in this story?

Writing News Releases. Is it important to adhere to what appear to be artificial rules (see page 152) for preparation of news stories? Anyone who ever has worked on the copy desk or in the news department of a newspaper, a magazine, or a broadcast station will verify that it is. You must assume that your release competes for space both with staff-written stories and with releases from professional public relations and publicity organizations. The "uniform" your story wears helps qualify it for consideration.

As an absolute rule, it is better to telephone a story to news media than to handwrite it, to prepare it badly because of the pressure of time, or to

FROM: Lewis-Nelson-Kahn   FOR: Azteca Corn Products Corp.
             410 N. Michigan Ave.
             Chicago, Illinois
CONTACT: Peggy Anderson
             (312) 644-6400

FOR IMMEDIATE RELEASE

        A tortilla for every man, woman, and child in Mexico.

        It's not the product of all the factories in Mexico, working
day and night for a year. To the surprise of almost no one in
the food industry, it's less than a month's output at a single
food processing plant in Chicago.

        The tortilla, Mexico's most staple food item, has invaded
the Midwest with strength.

        Azteca Corn Products Corp., Chicago, a major supplier of
both corn and flour tortillas to this region, now prepares nearly
15 million tortillas every week in a gleaming, modern plant in
suburban Stickney that is far removed from the rough stone wheels
that for hundreds of years have ground corn in Mexico.

        The growth of popularity of tortillas in the Chicago area
is geared to the increasing popularity of ethnic foods in general.
According to Arthur Velasquez, youthful president of Azteca, a
recent market survey showed that 46 percent of the 21-40 age
group prefer Mexican food to any other ethnic specialties.

                                    -more-

*Publicity information is properly transferred to the news media by a
professionally written news release.*

Rules for Writing News Releases

- Identify the sender. From whom is the release? Who is the individual to contact should the news medium want additional information?

- Double space all news stories.

- For stories whose significance cannot be stated in the first sentence, suggest a headline treatment by putting a few words at the top of the story, in capitals, that tell what the story is about.

- Indicate a release date in capital letters, just above the story itself. If the story is to be released at once, the wording is "FOR IMMEDIATE RELEASE." If it has a specific release date, the wording is similar to: "FOR RELEASE AFTER 1 PM JUNE 15, 19——."

- If the story is exclusively for one medium—one publication, for instance, or one radio station—indicate this instead of or in addition to the release date: "SPECIAL TO BAKERS' WEEKLY."

- If the story covers more than a page, write "more" at the bottom of each page. At the end of the story, write "end" or use a symbol such as "###." (The numerals, "30," used to indicate the end of copy, belong to old newspaper usage, and they are out of place in a news release.)

- IMPORTANT: After writing the story, go over it again to remove any puff adjectives that might have crept into it.

- Spell out numbers from one to ten, then use numerals from 11 up. Avoid starting a sentence with a number—but if you must, spell it out, regardless of what it is.

- Don't guess at dates or figures that a careful researcher might question. This laziness not only will send your story into the wastebasket, but will gain you the unhappy reputation of a fiction writer in an area devoted to facts.

- When sending news stories to broadcast media, be even more certain that the style is tight, bright, and breezy, and be certain to word it the way people talk, not the way they write. The story that a newspaper might begin, "A New York jeweler today exhibited a piece of cut glass as expensive as a diamond," probably would achieve more success as a broadcast news story if it were worded, "Next time someone ribs you about that fake ring on your finger, you have a comeback. A local jeweler says the Hope diamond is no more valuable than the glass of his window—provided that glass is cut in a certain way."

use improper writing techniques. However, a written release, properly done, is preferable.

If a story is really newsworthy and time does not permit preparation of a formal news release, telegrams are a potent way to get attention. But this approach must be used sparingly: once you have the reputation of yelling for attention and attempting to make an unimportant story seem important, you have put a barrier between yourself and the news media which will be almost impossible to overcome.

Handling News Photos. A photo will draw attention to your story and you may want to submit one with the release. If you do so, be sure it is a very sharp glossy print. In years past, 8 by 10 photographs were standard. Today, 5 by 7 prints, which are less expensive to produce, are acceptable almost everywhere.

The cutlines or captions for photographs should be typed, double spaced, on the bottom of a sheet of paper. Then the paper is glued with rubber cement to the back of the photograph, leaving the typed cutline below the photograph. The typed portion is then folded forward, covering the bottom front of the photograph.

Be sure to include all the important information in the cutline. Occasionally the news story will not be used—but the photograph will, with its descriptive cutline.

Remember to include identifications from left-to-right, should your photograph include a group of people. Although a publication may not demand it for its own coverage, a good rule to follow is to identify everyone in a photograph who is identifiable.

A photograph of an individual, used to announce a promotion, appointment, or change in position, can be a simple head shot. But the professional man whose photograph accompanies a story about a professional accomplishment should be shown in action.

Reproducing News Releases

Most news stories are not sent to only a single outlet. The same story may be sent to several outlets or to several hundred.

The accepted procedure is to have a technique of reproduction that most closely duplicates original typing. This means that spirit duplicators ("ditto" machines), however speedy and simple to handle they may be, are not the machines to use for duplication of news stories. Mimeographing is satisfactory and is probably the most common method of duplication used. Important stories being sent to many outlets might be either multigraphed or printed by offset. Advances in dry-process electrostatic copiers have made these machines popular for low-quantity copies of news releases, although those machines that produce gray and grainy copies should not be used.

Mailing News Releases. When mailing news releases accompanied by photographs, use a stiffener to prevent the photo from being creased. A shirt cardboard is ideal for this purpose, although stiff corrugated cardboard is often used.

All news stories and news photos should be sent first class mail, with the envelope identified with something like "NEWS PHOTO—VALUELESS IF DELAYED."

Finding a Market for News Stories

You will find that the reaction to your news releases and photographs, depending on how interesting the information is and on how well the news fits the medium to which it is sent, will run from wild enthusiasm to total apathy. Remember that news releases represent up to nine-tenths of the mail received by every news medium every day—and know that you must reach both the right outlet and the right person.

Tons of news releases are discarded every day because they are sent to the wrong outlet—or to the wrong person at the right outlet. What are the targets? If the audience would be interested in the news you are offering, the medium is a likely outlet. Trade magazines, for instance, are devoted to news of a particular industry. If your story is both about that trade or industry and newsworthy, the chances of insertion are usually good. But be certain that the material you send to such publications matches their format and style. Obviously, a trade magazine that runs no news stories will not run yours. And be certain that your photographs are not just badly lit shots of two men shaking hands.

Any well-prepared release is addressed to a specific individual, the person with the job of sorting out such releases or the person with the authority to accept or reject your release. If his name is unknown and you cannot locate it, at least make sure the release is addressed to the proper title.

It is a simple matter to learn the name of the news editor, the feature editor, the entertainment editor, the society editor, the business editor, or any other editor of a community newspaper. At broadcast stations, there are not only the news personnel to contact but also the "personalities" who conduct programs that depend upon fresh material and interviews for their existence. Most trade publications include on their mastheads the names of the editorial executives, and these are the names to whom business news stories should be sent.

Merely sending a news release to *The American Baker* or to *Iron Age* is playing Russian roulette with a news story that might be interesting to the publication's readers—if the right person on the publication's staff sees it and decides to use it.

Major News Outlets. Should you, if you are a relatively small marketer, send your story to a major outlet: a wire service, perhaps, or a national news magazine? If the story has strength and interest, there is nothing to lose. Suppose you stage an event in which anyone with a washing machine more than 50 years old has a chance to win a new washer. This is feature material that might get wide coverage, depending on how it is handled. Properly handled, the promotion will not draw a blank.

Broadcast Coverage. If a development or change is an important one, it may justify television newsreel coverage or a feature interview. The news departments of broadcast stations look for events that are newsworthy; a phone call will bring an answer.

Sometimes the newsroom will reply, "Set it up for Thursday. If nothing else happens, we'll have a crew there at 11 o'clock." This means exactly what it says: the crew will be there—unless some bigger news breaks. The station's ultimate responsibility is to its audience, not to the supplier of handout news.

The Contact List. Who gets the news release? The city editor? The managing editor? The feature editor? The women's page editor? The sports editor? Smaller publications may have a single individual performing all these jobs. Larger publications are strongly departmentalized, and many news releases that might have been printed are lost because they are sent to the wrong person or department.

If you have any doubts, phone the publication, asking for the department you think might be most interested in the news release. Describe the story briefly, and ask whether the person or department might be interested. In some cases, this establishes a certain receptivity for the story. In other cases, you have picked the wrong department or person but are able to get a referral to the right outlet.

Prepare and maintain a contact list, changing it as individual newswriters and contacts are changed. This list should be classified by medium, name, position, and type of story. Within a single medium of communication, there may be outlets for several different types of stories. A marketer may have a list of news outlets and people to contact about trade stories, a different but often overlapping list for local-interest stories, and a third list of those interested in financial news.

The existence of such a list simplifies distribution of news stories, avoids the problem of forgetting to include an important outlet, and assures the best possible potential coverage of each release.

Staging Stunts

Sometimes news can be of a circus variety: a deliberate stunt. One Washington furrier advertised a mink coat for "1,500 potatoes" in a radio broadcast. Whether by prearrangement or not, someone showed up with

1,500 potatoes. The furrier argued that, in the vernacular, "potatoes" obviously meant "dollars." But, with microphones in front of him and television cameras whirring and a large number of reporters on hand, he finally honored his original announcement and delivered the coat in exchange for the potatoes—with publicity worth far more than $1,500.

This does not mean that you should think entirely in terms of stunts. It does suggest that showmanship can be the difference between a news item that gets buried in the wastebasket and one that blossoms into print. More important, showmanship can be the difference between an item the news media reject as unworthy and one in which they take an interest.

Holding a Press Conference

An occasion may arise in which circumstances or importance may dictate holding a press conference—that is, inviting members of the press to hear an announcement, see a new development, or meet someone important.

A press conference need not be held at your headquarters or office or store, although sometimes that can be effective. If you have no suitable conference or display area, or if it is difficult for those invited to get to your location, use a hotel suite or a public meeting area.

What reasons might there be for holding a press conference rather than submitting news in release form? There are three common ones:

- A demonstration or showing, such as of new fashions, automobiles, creative arts, or equipment.

- The introduction and interviewing of an important personality or trade leader.

- An announcement of special community or commercial interest and importance.

Keep a press conference informal until the announcement itself is made, regardless of the kind of news or the type of demonstration for which the press conference has been called. Too many amateurs stage press conferences that try to mirror those held by the President of the United States—but few marketers can produce correspondingly important or cataclysmic news. Creating an air of false importance usually will produce scanty attendance at the next press conference you try to hold.

Procedures. Depending on the time of day, coffee, hors d'oeuvres, or cocktails may be served. Regardless of refreshments, however, the conference itself should begin within 10 minutes of the appointed time. If for any reason there is an unavoidable short delay, the reason should be announced to those present.

Too many press conferences featuring "celebrities" (whom one writer has described as "people who are well known for their well-knownness") start as much as an hour late, because the celebrity, often through habit, arrives late. This can hurt the individual who has called the press conference. Starting late gives the impression that you consider the time of the news reporters who have come to hear your announcement without value. Consciously or unconsciously, a reporter may find that having his time wasted affects his reporting of the event.

If the news announcement is technical or contains many names or facts, it is a good policy to distribute fact-sheets or press kits. In fact, any announcement should be prepared in news release form, so that it can be distributed to those in attendance and sent to those media that did not send representatives. If a formal statement is to be read, have copies available if possible either before or after the statement is made (and expect more questions from the reporters if the copies are available in advance, for this gives them time to study the statement).

Any announcement or statement should be followed by a question-and-answer period. If you do not want to allow questions and do not have people on hand who can answer them, don't hold a press conference. The interest of the question-and-answer session is one of the most important reasons for using this means of communication.

Photographs should be available as requested. Usually a company prepares some photographs in advance, to be handed out with the press kit. Often a company may have a photographer on hand to take shots as requested by the reporters, who may not be accompanied by their own photographers. The expense is small compared to the value of the publicity earned if the photographs are used. (Occasionally it is practical to negotiate with a newspaper photographer present to buy extra prints of his photographs for dissemination to other media.)

If the news disseminated at a press conference could be transmitted just as easily by a news release, the conference should not have been called. Representatives of news media have no time to waste. For every press conference a reporter attends, he may turn down three, five, or ten others. If you want attendance, build and maintain a reputation of making your press conferences a solid source of hard, real news.

PUBLIC RELATIONS

A sound public relations program usually includes both internal relations and community relations. The larger the organization, the more important internal relations become. Larger companies, schools, trade unions, military organizations, branches of government, and civic groups usually have internal public relations problems that are caused by a lack of communications between those who run the organization and rank and file members.

A good rule to follow when planning any internal public relations program is this: Participation is more important than pamphlets.

The first thought that comes to mind when attempting to influence someone within a group is to use a spoken or written approach, either reasoning, demanding, or pleading for a favorable reaction. Such an approach is not always logically correct, if a company follows the concept that inviting participation by members or workers is more important than distributing pamphlets to them. Instead of distributing pamphlets and leaflets, which, although easy to do, may well be unsuitable for influencing a state of mind, a better method may be to hold a series of meetings or intramural contests or to give awards. It is unfortunately true that in many industrial and civic situations, those who need employee or member cooperation the most seem the least likely to get it. Part of the reason for this is the inevitable resentment felt by labor toward management or by rank and file members toward leadership. Inclusion of more people in the group's activities is often a powerful cure for resentment and misunderstanding.

For many businessmen, community relations begins and ends with donated merchandise or advertising in yearbooks. In most communities, far better opportunities for positive and worthwhile public relations exist. For example, a business organization can sponsor or supply prizes for a local art fair; scholarships; athletic teams; essay, athletic, or academic contests; or popular music presentations.

In addition, a number of "vertical" publics exist—special-interest groups bound together by one single common aspect. Senior citizens, ethnic groups, unemployed persons, business executives, young people, and veterans are examples of vertical groups that represent a positive opportunity for community relations. Seizing every opportunity to communicate with these groups can result in potent public relations for the alert company, which is not only aware of the existence of these vertical groups but sensitive to their viewpoints.

Some examples of public relations activities toward vertical publics are the following activities:

- Discounts to senior citizens

- Displays featuring ethnic groups (blacks, Indians, descendants of one particular country of origin)

- Employment clearinghouse for the unemployed

- Luncheons for business executives

- Career discussions for young people

- Special offers to veterans

The House Organ

House organs are publications issued by a business, an organization, or a community group; circulation may be totally "internal," in which case all copies are distributed to members of the group, or "external," in which case the house organ becomes an arm of the public relations campaign.

Among fund raising groups, house organs are especially popular, because they feature names and photographs of heavy contributors as well as illustrated stories of the operation of the charity itself. There are two philosophies determining the content of the house organs: (a) include what the readers will enjoy—news about themselves, entertainment, and controversial opinion—and (b) include what the sponsor of the house organ wants the readers to know—organization news, company objectives, management's point of view.

The ideal house organ serves both philosophies. But those who publish house organs should remember that such publications need not compete

SINGERSINGER SINGER SINGER SINGER
SINGER SINGER SINGER SINGER SINGER
SINGER SINGER SINGER SINGER SINGER
SINGER SINGER SINGER SINGER **NEWS**

FOR EMPLOYEES OF THE SINGER COMPANY, EXECUTIVE OFFICE

VOLUME 2/NO. 5

SINGER INTRODUCES NEW TOP-OF-THE LINE
"FUTURA" SEWING MACHINE, MODEL 900

More than 100 members of the press attended a preview showing last month of
Singer's new top-of-the line "Futura" sewing machine -- a unique home sewing
machine with the look of modern sculpture. Previewed in an art gallery setting
at Automation House in New York City, the gracefully streamlined sewing machine,
designated Model 900, combines clean, simple lines with the most advanced
sewing technology. Among the major features that distinguish this sewing
machine from all previous top-of-the line models are:

- A new functional design that incorporates a slant-arm to
  enlarge the sewing area, and dial controls at eye level
  that are concealed under a flip-up cover to protect them
  from dust and lint.
- One-step, built-in buttonholer that programs the machine
  to stitch the desired buttonhole.
- Color-coded dial controls, plus a stitch selection panel
  picturing the stitches to make choices quick and easy.
- Simplified one-motion threading from spool to needle --
  grooves replace the eyelets of regular machines to
  eliminate fumbling.

Priced at $449.95, the "Futura" sewing machine is now available at Singer
Sewing Centers across the country. It is being manufactured at the
Company's plants in Elizabeth, N.J., and Anderson, S.C., for both U.S. markets
and export markets in Europe.

SIGN UP FOR SAVINGS BONDS THROUGH
COMPANY'S PAYROLL SAVINGS PLAN

If you would like to have a nest egg stashed away for something special in
your life, why not join the Company's Payroll Savings Plan? And now that
U.S. Savings Bonds mature in less than six years, they will be ready when
you are. If you are not already buying bonds, you will have an opportunity
to sign up or increase your savings during the Company's 1973 "Take Stock in
America" campaign set for Monday, May 14. The campaign, which is also being
launched in Singer's other divisions and locations across the country, will
end Friday, May 18. William F. Schmied, group vice president, Aerospace &
Marine Systems Group, and Corporate Bond chairman of the Singer campaign, said
that he "believes in the Payroll Savings Program because it has far-reaching
results that benefit so many people. It strengthens the financial security
of the employee and bolsters the economy of our country." Currently, 15,000
Singer employees throughout the U.S. are buying bonds through Payroll Savings.
"We hope to be able to increase the number of bond purchasers and to encourage
employees to increase their regular investments," Mr. Schmied added. Remember
the date - May 14.

Courtesy of The Singer Co.

Internal public relations may be furthered by a house organ.

with general magazines for content. They should, rather, present a view-point, doing so in as entertaining and sprightly a method as can be achieved within the framework of their editorial content.

While the magazine format is most common among the major house organs, smaller companies quite regularly use a newsletter format, in which less attention is paid to production methods than to content.

Other Publications

The formal house organ is by no means the only type of publication that may be used in a public relations campaign. Others include comic books, maps, guidebooks, sponsored books, and "vanity" books.

Comic books are an especially powerful public relations tool because they are much more likely to be read than other types of publications. The comic book format is one that people accept as entertainment, and anything printed in this format, with typical comic book art and structure, can anticipate a more intensive and widespread reading than any other type of pamphlet or brochure. Good comic book art, while not as inexpensive as straight typesetting, is not as expensive as the better-quality illustration demanded by a more formal publication. While comic books usually require full-color printing, "hairline" register (the fitting of two or more printing images on the same sheet of paper in exact alignment with each other) is not required, and low-cost newsprint paper stock can be used except for the cover. When the story must be told, told simply, and told in the hundreds of thousands, comic books often are the ideal method.

Maps are advantageous not only because they represent multiple ex-posures (each time the map is used the message may be seen) but because the longevity of maps is far greater than that of typical promotional literature. There is no shortage of free road maps sponsored by the major oil companies; thus, the businessman who wants to compete by issuing a map that will be retained and used, instead of competing head on with these existing maps, should issue maps that show areas, locations, or information not singled out for attention by typical road maps. For example, a company might issue a map of good fishing areas, bicycle or horseback-riding paths, mobile home rest areas, or any type of specialty that might reflect, even indirectly, on the business being promoted.

Guidebooks have a value similar to that of maps: They may be used for a year or more. Typical guidebooks might show places to eat, specifying price and cuisine; recreational activities available geographically or chronologically; a list of discount shopping sources; hotels, motels, and auto routes; scenic wonders; or any content that might interest the public. A guidebook is not to be assembled without thought. If the guidebook is to benefit the sponsor, it should be unique and well researched.

Some companies sponsor the publication of paperback or even hardcover books. Too often, the subject matter of these books is of interest only to the company sponsoring them. A history of a company, unless peppered with anecdotes and human interest, appeals only to the vanity of the head of the company. On the other hand, a handbook of fashion and makeup, sponsored and published by a fashion or beauty aid manufacturer, can achieve wide distribution and demand.

"Vanity" books are those whose cost of publication is paid for by the authors, who simply want their words in print. A number of publishing houses exist by issuing such books, some of which have genuine merit and some of which have none. A businessman may not benefit from publication of a volume of poetry. He may, however, see a benefit in publishing a technical treatise that underscores his own position as an authority in his field.

Often a better approach than sponsored or vanity publishing is submitting an article to one of the trade magazines in the field. If the information is indeed of interest, the magazine may publish it; the individual then can have the article reprinted and enjoy the benefit of adding "As printed in (name of publication)."

DISPLAY

Display is a specialized form of sales promotion of particular importance to retailers. Any marketer who expects customers to come to his store to buy merchandise depends strongly on displays to advertise both his store's image and the merchandise that he has available.

Stores usually divide displays into two major categories: window displays and interior displays. Interior displays may be of a general nature, or they may be hard-hitting point-of-purchase tools intended to get customers to stop and buy.

Effective displays are no accident. Their design is a specialized art. Larger stores have well-paid display staffs who dress the windows and handle all the important interior displays, although the salespeople may be responsible for setting up small displays within departments. Even smaller stores often hire professional displaymen rather than risk an amateurish look in what may be the store's only display window.

The point-of-purchase displays used in mass-market outlets in general and in supermarkets in particular are delivered ready to install. They seldom are as elaborate as some of the permanent interior displays used in stores handling more general merchandise, such as department stores, but they have a hard-hitting impact that can boost the sales of the product they promote. Testing of point-of-purchase materials is a serious and highly sophisticated business.

Window Displays

Window displays are of particular importance to department and specialty stores, to variety stores, to any kind of retail outlet that wants to draw customers from among people who pass by the store. Supermarkets, on the other hand, use their windows simply for large price signs, since most food shopping is done on schedule rather than on impulse.

The first group of retailers, however, consider windows a valuable medium for advertising. The displays in a store's window are an attractive lure, drawing people over to look at the merchandise in the window and hopefully convincing them to enter the store. Windows frequently are used for institutional advertising as well as for displaying merchandise; institutional windows help build and maintain that all-important company image.

Merchandise Windows. When a store wants to use its windows to sell merchandise, the display features that merchandise. What constitutes an appropriate display of merchandise depends upon the store. A prestige-minded store may put a single fashion item in a window against an elaborate background, or it may concentrate on showing a new season's color or look rather than showing a collection of individual items. A discount store or a variety store, however, probably will stack its windows high with merchandise, each item with its price particularly prominent.

Arranging such displays may be a specialist's business, but it is up to the marketer to assure that the items shown in a window display are available in sufficient supply in the store. The window usually indicates where customers can find the items on display—and once the customers take the trouble to go into the store and find the right area, those items had better be there, in full assortment. Using a window to display items that are not stocked in sufficient depth in the store is as bad as picturing items in an advertisement that are not available at the store.

That marketer also should make sure that all salespeople know what the windows are featuring each day. Frequently a customer will come in and want to look at "a pair of shoes like those brownish flats in the corner of the window," and the salesperson had better know which ones the customer means. Ignorance at this point simply turns the customer away.

Institutional Windows. Sometimes window displays contain no merchandise, or if merchandise is displayed that merchandise is secondary to the theme of the window. Perhaps best known are the window displays set up for holiday seasons, such as Christmas and Easter, and those honoring such groups as the Red Cross or the Boy Scouts during the period of a fund drive.

Institutional windows are not intended to sell merchandise—but they do sell the image of the store as a community-minded organization. Smaller stores frequently are asked whether they will put some mention of local fund drives in their windows and are offered the display materials to do it with. Even devoting a portion of a store's only window to an institutional theme, if handled cleanly, can tie the store more closely to the community.

But the store that allows its windows to be a repository for any sign, announcement, poster, and display card announcing every charity, play, rummage sale, and sports event in town will achieve just the wrong reputation: the image is as slovenly as the window itself, and the attempt to participate to the hilt in community affairs builds an image of a messy, disorganized business. One answer to the constant clamor for free use of display windows is the allocation of a corner, neatly laid out and labeled, "This Week's Announcement." Those who want to use the space are told that a display card of a specific size, professionally lettered, will be considered, on a first-come, first-served basis.

Courtesy of Delman Shoes, New York, N.Y.

Merchandise may be appealingly included in an institutional display.

There is a distinct danger in having a place of business become known as a mecca for information. Serious customers can develop a dislike for the unbusinesslike bustle. Community relations are best served when the principles of common sense prevail.

Interior Displays

Interior displays are designed to get the customer's attention and sell merchandise. These displays are placed at convenient locations where the customer is able to look closely at the goods. These are the primary goals of interior displays:

- To establish a mood

- To help customers choose between styles and other variations within a particular line

- To identify a section or department

- To help customers locate advertised merchandise

- To help sell merchandise that has not been advertised

Interior displays are important both in stores that give customers considerable salesperson assistance and in stores that are primarily self-service. The types of displays, however, vary according to the type of store.

Stores well staffed with salespeople use interior displays to create an atmosphere, to decorate walls and corners, to identify the different areas in which merchandise can be found, and to help customers decide between different styles or variations. There is seldom anything of the hard-sell approach in these displays. They are aids to the selling process, not the primary method of selling. The sales presentation of the selling staff does that job.

Self-service stores, however, expect their interior displays both to identify and to sell. Displays direct customers to the right area—and then they sell: a particular product, a particular brand, a particular item.

Signs and Cards.   The most common point-of-purchase advertising device is the sign. It is basic identification—and a direct selling tool. It informs—and it encourages people to buy.

Some signs are designed to be taped or set in a window, to be viewed from the outside as the customer enters the store. Newer window signs have pressure-sensitive adhesive edges to simplify installation, because the biggest deterrent to the use of point-of-purchase materials usually is the difficulty in assembling, mounting, or displaying them.

Other signs are designed to be hung above shopping areas or set above displays. The unsupported sign invariably winds up on the floor, but companies specializing in the production of point-of-purchase devices have come up with some ingenious methods to keep this from happening.

Counter cards often are a problem, since the average counter has little display space. A good counter card not only will occupy little space (which need not reduce its overall size: it can sit on a narrow base, which occupies little of the counter area but stands tall and thin), but it also may well act as a rack to hold the item featured, if that item is a small one.

Signs can be die-cut in the shape of human figures, rocket ships, cars, boats, giant blowups of the product itself—anything that will attract attention. Even though display space always is at a premium, and even though this problem is most intense in the stores that offer the highest volume, a clever, eye-catching display sign may be well worth every inch of space given to it if only because so many competing displays are so uninteresting.

Racks. Display racks are popular point-of-purchase devices because they serve a dual purpose: they display a product and provide space for self-service stocking of that product as well. For example, most greeting card manufacturers offer free display racks to stores that agree to give them good floor positions. Unlike the greeting card racks of the 1950s, which often hid the cards or made it difficult for a customer to pick one, the greeting card racks of the 1970s are wide open, offering maximum display and ease of attention and commanding that attention. They also reflect the understanding that midfloor space is easier to obtain than wall space, because many of them stand on a pedestal, offering 360-degree inspection.

Such display racks, which are convenient and which separate their merchandise from other similar merchandise in the store, are perfect for consignment items, since there is no intermingling of the stock and the retailer has no display problem. A supplier may offer to a retail store a rack of novelties, nylon hose, pet supplies, light bulbs, or automotive accessories. The store does nothing but supply space for the rack. The owner of the rack sets it up, stocks it, checks it regularly and keeps it fully stocked, and the store pays for only those items that have been sold from the display.

Other Point-of-Purchase Devices. A growing number of point-of-purchase devices are on the product itself, since in many stores no other display space exists. For example, a soft drink bottler might devise a display that

The many varieties of point-of-purchase displays in this photograph reduce counter space but stimulate impulse sales.

fits around the neck of one of the bottles in a six-pack. Printed in Day-Glo inks, the display will bring attention to the entire area.

In situations in which the floor space is not so crowded, ideas can be more imaginative. One car dealer filled an automobile with pennies. A farm equipment dealer converted an entire wall into a movie screen, aiming at it a projector that mixed cartoon segments with hard-sell business films.

The ceiling has received the most recent large-scale attention in the point-of-purchase device field, because this is the last large open space available in many retail establishments. Mobiles and hanging displays and signs have become popular. Retailers have found clever ways of affixing them to the ceiling.

Inducements and Incentives. Contests and promotions help increase the longevity and use of point-of-purchase devices. It is common practice for a manufacturer or distributor to offer prizes for "the best use of a point-of-sale display." The retailer is asked to take a photograph of the display and send it to the wholesaler or the manufacturer; he becomes a contestant who might win a prize, instead of a nonparticipant who might not feature that particular product.

That such inducements and incentives are offered at all is acknowledgement that the demand for point-of-purchase space in mass-merchandise stores exceeds the supply of space in such stores. Nevertheless, some shortsighted manufacturers continue to supply difficult-to-assemble displays that the most dedicated model-airplane enthusiast would find a problem, and the alleys behind supermarkets become the only place where these displays are seen.

The supplier who can ask that his own salesmen set up the displays will have far better luck. However, if a supplier offers such services to one customer, he must make them available to all customers who request them; the Robinson-Patman Act forbids discrimination by a supplier among his customers.

Studies constantly underscore the importance of point-of-purchase devices in selling. Despite the per-unit cost and the difficulty of implementing their use, point-of-purchase materials enjoy major attention from thoughtful manufacturers. Newer devices are motorized; some of these displays are even triggered to go into action when a customer crosses a photoelectric beam. Catching the customer's attention is all-important, and manufacturers and retailers alike cannot afford to ignore that important instant when a customer is within range of the product.

EXHIBITS

Exhibits are displays used by companies at trade shows and conventions to give their products maximum exposure. Because space at such shows is expensive, some of the larger companies may have elaborately designed display units that take a day or more to assemble, contain a multiplicity of electronic devices, operate on several levels, require a number of people to man the exhibit booth, and represent a real logistics problem to transport. The smaller company cannot compete in flamboyance with such exhibits— but it can mount a display that is practical and attractive and adheres to these principles of usefulness that make running an exhibit a pleasure instead of a dreaded chore.

- The display should be designed to be shipped in one or two master containers. Some well-designed displays fold along hinges so that the back of the display walls become the shipping container.

- The display should not weigh tons. Modern materials such as Fiberglas, Masonite, and lightweight plastics are standard with most of the companies that produce displays. Some of the best exhibit displays are lightweight enough to be carried by one person.

- The display should not require complicated electric installation. Even though an audiovisual unit, polarizing light effects, or a flashing sign may be involved, these should be designed for automated operation. It usually is necessary to use union labor in setting up any elaborate electrical system, because the exhibit halls in large cities usually have union contracts— but there is no law that keeps the salespeople manning the booth from plugging in a wire.

- The display should be self-standing. Accomplishing this is as simple as having end braces with flanges that fit into flat shoes. Convention managers are painfully familiar with home-made displays that teeter, sway, and threaten to collapse— and these are not the kinds of displays that make a prospective customer feel relaxed and receptive.

- The display should not be so crowded with different elements that visitors cannot enter it. At most shows, the displays butt against the aisle; if there are too many parts to the display and it stands flush against the aisle, visitors are kept outside, making lengthy and persuasive conversation with them difficult.

- The display should have a logical, attractive, accessible place for literature. Information about the company is the first goal of the display, and making it difficult for the passerby to pick up sales literature defeats the impact of the display.

A unit for a trade-show exhibit should be portable, self-standing, and self-lighted and should feature the company name.

Courtesy of Exhibitgroup
New York Inc.

- The display should be colorful, not drab. Too many displays constructed of dark brown perforated Masonite remain that same dark brown color. Competition for attention is the rule, not the exception, and color and brightness help attract attention.

- The display should be self-lighted. Many display areas are not adequately lighted, and adding lights can involve paying special union labor. If the display has built-in swingaway lights, the problem is avoided.

- The display should utilize every inch of the amount of exhibit space rented. Most booths at trade shows are sold in multiples of 10 feet. The standard exhibit booth is 10 feet long; a double booth is 20 feet long. If the display is 8 feet long, bring along some chairs for visitors so that those extra 2 feet are put to use.

- The display should feature the company name prominently. This is what the visitors to the booth are expected to remember. In most cases, it is impossible to make too much of the name, to display it too prominently, or to repeat it too often within the booth. Remember that the display is a form of advertising.

- The display should make use of air space. Mobiles and other hanging additions to the display can catch the eye from a distance. Inflated balloons, if permitted (some trade shows forbid such displays but many others do not), give a competitive edge to the exhibit because they can be seen from farther away than a sign.

AUDIOVISUAL TOOLS

Audiovisual promotional materials are widespread. To some companies, producing a sales or public relations film is as routine a project in the 1970s as was turning out sales literature in the 1950s. The art of television commercials was discussed in an earlier chapter—but audiovisual possibilities do not end there. Audiovisual techniques are being used even more widely as tools for salesmen, in the home office, in the field, in exhibits, and in the store.

The one development that has made widespread use of audiovisual materials practical is the availability of equipment that makes close-to-professional results possible without requiring professional studio setups. Thousands of effective audiovisual presentations are produced every year by businessmen with no technical knowledge. Some of the results rival studio-produced jobs in every way except cost.

Filmstrips

Years ago, the first generation of filmstrip (sometimes called sound-slide film) viewers watched an interminably long series of still photos that changed when the operator heard a loud "beep" on the accompanying recording and pushed a button that changed the picture. Today's filmstrip projectors are largely automatic, advancing the picture through the impulse note of an inaudible signal. While adding the automatic signal requires a professional sound studio, shooting the still photos and narrating the original sound are not technically demanding.

Each picture in a filmstrip is the same size as a full-frame 35mm motion picture frame, usually all the picture area in a four-perforation field (totally unrelated to the usual eight-perforation 35mm still photographs that you take on your home cameras, except that the film itself is the same size). Many new cartridge-type filmstrips are 16mm.

A filmstrip must be animated—that is, put into a single strip of film in which the pictures appear in proper order. Animating the film is a simple procedure but one that requires professional equipment. An animating cameraman usually charges by the frame. A filmstrip can be animated from 35mm transparencies, color or black-and-white photographs of any size, artwork, or any combination of these. Titles and numbers can be superimposed on the individual frames. The very rapid picture advance possible on today's projectors even makes it possible to produce such interesting effects as a picture in which a question mark suddenly seems to appear; this is done by showing in sequence first the picture itself and then that same picture with the question mark superimposed on it.

When producing a filmstrip, an average of one picture change every 10 seconds is a good one to maintain. This timing gives each frame a chance to receive proper attention and yet avoids the boredom of having the same frame in front of the viewers for too long. Six pictures a minute means that a 10-minute film would be about 60 frames. That length of film, even with leaders and focus-frame, will total no more than 5 feet.

There are two advantages to filmstrips:

First, production is easy, since the sequence of the pictures can be prearranged and any one picture can be added or dropped while the filmstrip is being assembled. Product shots not easily photographed or not locally available sometimes can be picked up from other sources, such as sales literature or manufacturers' promotional photographs.

Second, as a general rule filmstrip projectors are less expensive than motion picture projectors, and prints of the strip-plus-recording (either disc or tape) also cost less. With 16 frames per 35mm foot or 40 frames per 16mm foot, a typical filmstrip may use only 5 or 6 feet of film.

35mm Slides

Great advances have been made in the last few years in projectors for 35mm slides (sometimes called 2 by 2 slides, since when mounted for projection the outside measurement of the mount is 2 inches square). In the past these usually were regarded as amateur equipment on which a neighbor might show transparencies of his trip to Tahiti, but today's projectors are designed for business use.

Newer 35mm slide projectors offer a choice of automatic advance devices. They can be preset so that each slide is shown for a specific number of seconds, or they may have a pushbutton advance that does not require the slides to be handled. Some units have electronic synchronization with tape-cartridge sound, making the presentation competitive with a filmstrip (although not as trouble-free, since each slide is separate, rather than being one frame on a strip of film). Automatic dissolve devices can link two projectors together.

Most often, 35mm slides are cardboard or glass-mounted transparencies that have been photographed on a 35mm still camera. For quantity use, it is a simple photo laboratory procedure to make 35mm slides from transparencies of a larger size as well as from original slides.

Since 35mm slide projectors are far less expensive than motion picture or filmstrip projectors and since slides are easier to prepare than film footage, their use can be far more widespread. A businessman who is at all familiar with the simplicity of preparing a slide presentation never should let a window or display area lie unused. Putting a projector and a small screen in that space and letting the slides run automatically turns dead space into a lively selling display.

EVR and Videocassettes

EVR (electronic video recording) has been hailed as the most important electronic teaching advance of the 1970s. The system is a method of playing either unperforated 8mm film or videotape through any standard television receiver, thus eliminating the need for expensive projection equipment.

Whether the videocassette will realize the potential claimed for it by its proponents depends on whether the giant companies that dominate the educational films and audiovisual equipment fields embrace it. Not until both equipment and films themselves become plentiful will costs drop. However, as videocassettes are improved, similar improvements in standard 8mm and 16mm projection equipment to remove weight, add efficiency, lower costs, and widen potential uses are being made.

A major obstacle to the rapid adoption of prerecorded videocassettes has been the inability of the manufacturers of equipment to agree on a standard format. Those using the film technique point out the low cost of mass reproduction of prints; those using videotape point out that tapes can be erased and rerecorded.

Such bickering has slowed adoption of units by large industrial and commercial users. The confusion is similar to that which beset the phonograph industry when 78-, 45-, and 33-rpm records were competing with each other for public favor. In the case of the videocassette, a further complication is that no single existing unit can play the product of more than one of the available methods (as a phonograph can play all three speeds, since the recordings themselves are of a single type of manufacture). An indication of negative public reaction to videocassette industry confusion is that in mid-1973, the major manufacturer of consumer cassettes filed for bankruptcy. But even as this occurred, electronics industry spokesmen repeated their faith in the ultimately bright future of the medium.

The huge potential of the prerecorded videocassette market is enhanced by the availability of rental equipment and even more by the availability of rental cassettes. The owner or renter of the playback unit also can rent

Courtesy of Sony Corp. of America

The videocassette is an audiovisual tool which has enormous potential for the advertiser and the salesman.

a feature film, sports event, or instructional cassette, which he can play through his television set. Enthusiastic proponents of this system claim that it will make other training and entertainment media obsolete eventually.

When videotape was first introduced, similar claims were made: that the development would make motion pictures obsolete. Instead, new uses for film were born in the new medium, and both sides prospered.

Since the electronic picture is actually 525 separate lines of "scan" (625 lines in some foreign-made systems), its quality, except when compared with other images on the television tube itself, is not equal to that of normal color film projected on a standard screen or even on a white wall. However, through EVR and videocassettes, multiple-set coverage can mean storewide or officewide distribution of audiovisual materials on an instant basis without having to bring the people together in one place. The same results are possible through videotape, but ultimately EVR could be a less troublesome and less costly procedure.

In an electronic age, mass communications change rapidly. The use of the television monitor to reach and influence people and the use of electronic devices as advertising-communications weapons are in their infancy. We can expect to see new devices and improvements in existing devices each year, and both should challenge the imagination and create new avenues of advertising and sales promotion.

The videocassette is one of those improvements. It has a use potential that no existing competitor at present can approach. For example, one supplier has indicated that he will make 30 hours of programming of various types—entertainment, enrichment, indoctrination—available to hospitals. Male patients, who traditionally have an increase in "discomfort calls" during the hours when the women's programs dominate television, will have packaged entertainment available for them; the patient scheduled for an operation will have both preoperative and postoperative procedures explained on the screen of his television set.

The logic, ease, and advantage over conventional projection techniques are obvious.

Tape and Disc Recording

The development of cartridge and repeater-playback equipment has made possible the use of recorded sales materials for every type of business at very low cost.

One real estate developer, for example, uses a prerecorded message on a 45-rpm phonograph playback unit in each room of his model homes. These units are set to keep repeating their messages, and they eliminate the need for continuous personal explanations by salesmen on heavy-traffic days. At a lake property development, a continuous cartridge-playback unit is connected to loudspeakers concealed in the trees, and the story of the development, together with comments about the scenic views, is presented throughout the day.

Many a retailer has learned the value of a tiny (usually about 5 inches) weatherproof loudspeaker attached above a display window, with a taped commentary drawing passersby to the window. Sometimes entrepreneurs who regularly use recorded carols at Christmastime to intensify the seasonal spirit on their premises forget about the value of this approach during other times of the year.

Most automatic phonographs will play the same message over and over again when the changer arm is flipped to the side. This makes possible repeated recordings over a simple system that may involve nothing more than attaching a speaker to the phonograph. Repeater cartridges are practically foolproof and can play for days without maintenance.

Phonograph records themselves serve an additional purpose when mailed to customers and prospects. Playing these records is often far more painless than reading a lot of printed sales literature—and unusual enough an approach so that the records usually are played, not discarded.

The Telephone

Hello, Mrs. Brown? I'm calling for the Smith Department Store. Our private sale for our regular customers is being held next Monday, Tuesday, and Wednesday. Since there will be no general announcement about this sale, we did want to be sure that you knew about it.

Mrs. Brown, this is Jane Jacobs from the Jacobs Charm School. I noticed an inquiry from you about your daughter—you returned the coupon from one of our ads. May I ask you how old your daughter is, and what her dress size is?

Mrs. Brown, this is Rose Dominique from the Industrial Plumbers Company. We need information from representative homeowners. Do you have a water filter on your water line into the kitchen?

Mr. Brown, this is Roy Smith from the Barstow Company in Hodgeville. I'm calling you because I plan to be in your area next Monday and Tuesday.

Mrs. Brown, this is Roy Carletti. I'm running for a council seat in this ward, and I'd be interested in knowing what you think about the suggestion that city bus fares be raised.

These examples could be joined by thousands more, each demonstrating the use of the telephone as a sales and advertising instrument. People who never could be reached or influenced in any other way can be motivated by a phone call, especially one that appears to be long distance.

The "canned pitch" is much in vogue among telephone mass-sales organizations, such as those that sell newspaper subscriptions, house siding, and real estate, and those that are trying to raise funds for various causes. While, obviously, a prepared sales talk is preferable to a totally ad lib and unprepared performance, it is equally obvious that after about 20 calls the freshness and spontaneity tend to dissipate, leaving the words flat and without conviction. Perhaps the best approach is to have the selling points carefully listed, but to ad lib the discussion of them.

Since the telephone represents a one-to-one approach to advertising and sales promotion—one salesman to one customer—it is no substitute for mass advertising in terms of cost. However, there is one strong argument in its favor: its results can be spectacular.

One way of cutting telephone costs is to use the various services available from the telephone companies. The various Bell, General Telephone, and independent companies, for example, offer WATS (wide area telephone service) to businessmen, a service that charges a bulk-amount rate for long-distance calls to specific areas. One type of WATS applies to calls within a given state; another covers regional areas; another covers calls throughout the entire continental United States except for the state in which the calls are originating; another makes possible calls throughout the country either on a total-number-of-phone-hours basis or on an unlimited basis; another covers incoming calls from anywhere in the country.

Using WATS lines removes some of the inhibitions many marketers may have about using the telephone for sales promotion. These lines can be valuable even to the company whose customer list is less than 100 names long, if those customers are spread throughout a region or throughout the country.

Psychologically, there is a great advantage: few businessmen will reject a long-distance call; many of those same businessmen will refuse to see a salesman or respond to a published ad.

Some areas offer residential subscribers unlimited local calls. In such cases, businessmen often advertise for women to work in their own homes as telephone solicitors. In the major metropolitan areas, often unlimited service is available only to suburban residents.

The single most important rule for using the telephone effectively: Have something to say, and word it so that it seems as beneficial to the listener as possible.

A second important rule: Even though this may be the fiftieth call of the day, look at it from the point of view of the person receiving the call and be as cheerful and spontaneous as though it were the first call you placed. Keep a note in front of you: "Be happy and sincere."

The Yellow Pages

An advertisement in the Yellow Pages represents the major portion of the promotional budget for many small businessmen. These same businessmen, forgetting that they depend upon this form of advertising for their expansion, often allow the salesmen for the Yellow Pages to write their advertising copy, which then imitates that of their competitors.

The Yellow Pages differs from conventional print and broadcast media in that there is no such thing as a noncompetitive ad, except in the smallest towns. Every listing is compared with those around it.

While salesmen for the Yellow Pages often offer sound and valuable advice, their job is to sell you advertising. Gauge all of their suggestions with this idea in mind.

The principal rule of Yellow Pages advertising parallels that of other media: The ad should reflect the state of mind of the reader, not that of the writer.

Other rules for using the Yellow Pages are these:

- "Experience" is a key word. If the company does not have a formidable history, a key executive does. Feature that.

- Give the business a local flavor. Specify the communities served, and, if possible, have a local phone number in each.

- Some Yellow Pages publishers restrict claims and guarantees. It is better to say nothing than to make a weak claim.

- Be specific. "One-hour service" is far superior to "fast service."

- Use heavy borders for every ad regardless of size.

There is no place for a jaded or tired approach in any sales promotion. The marketer whose sales promotion methods seem tired will find that customers in turn gradually grow tired of buying from him—but the marketer who works at making his sales promotion methods seem fresh has the best chance of holding customers and winning new ones.

NOW, APPLY WHAT YOU'VE LEARNED

Test your ability to organize and execute a public relations program, to design displays, and to handle an audiovisual program, based on the information in this chapter.

1. You manufacture machine tools. Your company has produced a new machine that in 2 minutes can change molds to form plastic shapes of almost any dimension.

   a. Plan a public relations and publicity campaign to introduce this item.

   b. Write a news release about this machine for trade publications.

   c. Write a news release about this machine for consumer publications.

2. Prepare a local consumer-media contact list for news stories about your own business.

3. You plan to exhibit uniforms and blazers at the trade show of The National Restaurant Association. Make a rough design of a 10 by 10-foot display booth.

4. You operate a fried chicken carry-out restaurant. Plan a complete promotion for Valentine's Day.

5. Write a complete telephone sales talk to be used for evening unsolicited phone calls to develop appointments to sell half-acre lots in Arizona for $995.

6. Describe the first 10 frames of a 60-frame filmstrip to be used to sell automobile insurance.

7. Submit an outline for a videotape, EVR, or videocassette program to teach hotel-motel management.

8. As a building contractor, you are opening a housing development—Shangri-La. Using all the methods described in this chapter, plan a rounded, powerful promotional campaign to sell homes in this development.

9. Design a back-to-school window display for a menswear store and for a drugstore.

10. You are an exterminator. Your company is new, but you've worked in this field for 20 years. You feature round-the-clock emergency service. Design a quarter-page Yellow Pages ad for your company.

CHAPTER SIX

Planning and Evaluation

The days in which the inept dropout was put in the advertising department of his father's firm because "he can't do us any harm there" are long past. Today, advertising and sales promotion are recognized as crucial marketing tools. The businessman of the 1970s understands the importance of carefully planning every feature of an ad, every aspect of a sales promotion effort. He knows the importance of making every cent in his advertising and sales promotion budget count.

Remember the basic rule of advertising:

> *The most effective advertising or sales promotion is the one that reaches, at the lowest possible cost, the largest number of people who can and will buy what you have to sell.*

The rule is really a challenge: How do you reach these people? What do you tell them? In an age when customers are surrounded, saturated, and battered by advertising and sales promotion, which motivators induce action?

The student of advertising and sales promotion knows that the answers he finds are only temporarily right and may not apply tomorrow. He should be determined that tomorrow he will, with an open mind and a facile imagination, try to get a new set of answers to fit whatever new situation or opportunity has arisen.

In advertising and sales promotion, as in any other professional field, there is no short road to knowledge. But there are ways that the marketer

184

who is not a professional advertising man or sales promotion expert can build his knowledge of advertising and sales promotion and thus can increase his ability to compete successfully. In addition to the techniques already discussed, he can learn:

- What professional assistance he can find, and where.

- How to gauge and use trends.

- How to keep his reading up to date—and why he should do so.

- How to collect research information—and why it is important.

- How to develop a logical advertising and sales promotion budget.

The world of communications is changing rapidly, and there are many new methods and techniques today's and tomorrow's marketer can use to win business. No one can say truthfully that he is an expert in all the facets of advertising and sales promotion—but learning the basic rules that guide experts as well as beginners and knowing where and when to seek expert help will make your business more successful, more competitive, and more profitable.

PROFESSIONAL ASSISTANCE

In planning advertising and sales promotion, the marketer often should think of himself as a general contractor, hiring subcontractors who possess specialized skills and knowledge. He has the ultimate responsibility and control for the advertising or sales promotion effort or campaign, but he needs professional assistance to make that job a success.

Four separate groups of professionals are of particular importance to you as marketer-contractor. Each has the advantage of knowledge of methods, materials, and new developments within a specific field. These groups are the graphic arts specialists, the printers, the space and time salesmen, and the advertising agencies.

Graphic Arts Specialists

Both art studios and individual artists will know the important new trends in layout, design, and illustration. They will have samples of both traditional and new typefaces. If you explain your needs properly, they can match art style and layout to the customer audience you are seeking.

Art is the one aspect of advertising and sales promotion in which the average marketer is least likely to achieve proficiency—but this does not mean that the buyer of commercial art should leave all decisions to the art studio or artist. Careful directions given to the art studio or the individual artist inevitably result in finished art that better reflects the intention of the entire promotion, rather than in art that represents the personal preference of one particular studio or artist.

Art Studios. Every major metropolitan market has art studios whose names are listed in the Yellow Pages of the telephone directory. Call them and ask to see samples of the work they do. Most art studios employ "outside men," salesmen who carry samples of the work done by various artists within the studio.

The advantage of dealing with a studio is that you can choose from a number of talents and art styles. The disadvantage is that, since the studio overhead is a cost factor and since the outside man is paid on a commission basis, the same art job often will cost more, sometimes considerably more, when done by a studio than it would if done by a free-lance artist contacted directly.

Artists. A classified ad in the help-wanted columns of the local newspaper usually will unearth several free-lance artists who will work, either at home or in your office, on your art jobs. In any such relationships, a flat-fee basis is preferable to a per-hour basis, if only because it eliminates some of the arguments that inevitably arise.

If you are a consistent advertiser, it may pay you to have a full-time artist who, when not working on ads, can design sales literature and handle other facets of sales promotion. Some groups of businessmen share an artist; two or three noncompeting business organizations use his time and pay his salary equally.

Printers. Seldom does one meet a printer who does not claim to be an expert in advertising and sales promotion. Sometimes such a claim is well justified, since printers are constantly exposed to competitive creative ideas.

Often a printer can offer advice about the kind of paper that should be used for a mailer, the colors to use, and the weight to which the mailing should adhere. If cooperative, he can save you considerable money. Printers necessarily know about recent changes in postal laws and regulations. They also should be familiar with mechanical tricks (such as dissolving paper, iridescent inks, and aromatic effects) that might brighten your promotional techniques.

Where printers often fall short is in their unthinking overuse of the supplies they may have on hand or the techniques with which they are most familiar. Sometimes the result of this shortcoming is a plethora of mailers, for instance—for you, for your competition, and for almost anyone else who uses that particular printer—printed on the same paper stock, utilizing the same typefaces, and even using the same type of fold.

This is one reason for collecting samples of good promotional printing jobs, even if they are totally unrelated to your own field. Not only do they stimulate the imagination of your printer and yourself, they also serve as an excellent base for obtaining competitive printing estimates.

In smaller markets, the printer may serve as advertising counsel as well as supplier. In fact, he may be the printer handling the community newspaper, using his presses on down days for commercial printing jobs. Like the artist, his talents should be measured and accepted in those areas in which they are more professional and skilled than your own.

Space and Time Salesmen

The sales representatives of advertising media can be an exceptionally potent source of ideas, not only because they may well know what your competitors' advertising plans are but, more important, because they themselves deal in the competitive sale of media.

From his weekly rounds, the newspaper space salesman knows in a generalized way which sections of the paper pull best for a particular business and which times of the year that business uses the most space. A broadcast salesman will know which shows reach the particular audience you may want. These salesmen gather this information from the complaints they may hear, if from no other source—but more positively, they instinctively recognize patterns of advertising that are repeated each year and therefore must have some seeds of success in them.

However, you should recognize that these salesmen's first loyalty is to their newspaper, trade paper, or broadcast station, not to you. They function best when transforming anything they know into ammunition for a sales argument: "We'll sell you spots for $3; the other station charges $9—and even if they had three times the audience we have, which is laughable, we'd be a better buy!"

Every word of this may be true, but none of it reflects a genuine attempt to merchandise what you have to sell. It is a bald and simple attempt to sell time. What might do you some good would be to try to get some concrete information about the type of audience reached, the cost of reaching those people, and perhaps an indication that the advertising outlet was used successfully in a similar campaign for someone else.

This does not mean that you should wait until a competitor has pretested the medium; too many businessmen wait to learn what their competitor is doing and thus are always in a "me too" position. Rather, it means that claims from media representatives should be weighed in the light of the realization that no matter how many free lunches are bought and no matter how many theater tickets are sent, this just is part of a job: to sell advertising space or time. What you want to find out is whether what is offered is sensible for you.

But space and time salesmen do know what goes on promotionally within your sphere of business. They know whether, within their own medium, multiple smaller ads are preferable to a few big ads. They know whether they can prevail upon their production people to put together the ad, which would be a moneysaver for you. And they may even become your publicity department, by transmitting a good idea for editorial coverage to the appropriate people in their organization.

Advertising Agencies

An advertising agency is supposed to represent you, not the advertising media, and therefore such an organization is capable of giving you unprejudiced advice and service in marketing communications.

A newspaper space salesman may help the advertiser to interpret a rate card in order to take advantage of the lower rates given for bulk advertising.

ADVERTISING RATES

OPEN LOCAL, POLITICAL, AMUSEMENT
SUNDAY or WEDNESDAY, per column inch..$2.90
DAILY, per column inch $2.40

TIME RATES—PER DAY
2 Consecutive Days, per column inch......$2.00
3 Consecutive days, per column inch......$1.80
1 Month, 26 Consecutive days,
   per column inch.....................$1.40
(Add 50c for Sunday or Wednesday per column inch)

BULK CONTRACT RATES

WRITTEN CONTRACT ONLY

USED WITHIN 1 YEAR OF DATE OF CONTRACT

	Daily	SUN. or WED.
130 column inches, per column inch	1.75	2.25
260 column inches, per column inch	1.35	1.85
520 column inches, per column inch	1.30	1.80
780 column inches per column inch	1.25	1.75
1040 column inches, per column inch	1.20	1.70
1560 column inches, per column inch	1.15	1.65
2080 column inches, per column inch	1.10	1.60
4160 or more column inches, per column inch	1.05	1.55

EXPANDED
SUNDAY-WEDNESDAY ISSUES

APPLICABLE TO LOCAL
CONTRACT ADVERTISERS ONLY

20,000 GUARANTEED CIRCULATION

2-DAY COMBINATION
SUNDAY in combination with Monday
or Tuesday

WEDNESDAY in combination with Thursday
or Friday
(Must be within same calendar week)

ADD 35c TO RATE

NO COPY CHANGES

However, some businessmen fear agencies because of misunderstandings about their cost structure and the way they function. Deciding whether or not to use an agency can be troublesome; choosing one, if you do decide to use one, should be handled carefully.

How to Pay an Advertising Agency.   Agencies are compensated in one of two ways: commissions or fees. Almost all national advertising media will pay an agency a 15 percent commission for ads placed by it. For example, an ad in a trade paper which costs $100 will cost you that $100 whether you place the ad direct or whether an agency places it for you. If the agency places the ad, however, it pays $15 less, or $85, to the trade paper. Thus, since your cost is the same, use of an agency can actually represent an extra bank of brainpower, drawing no salary at all, on your staff.

Commissions on printed work or other materials bought on the outside by the agency are figured by that agency at 17.65 percent of the net cost, which becomes 15 percent of the gross cost. For example, an agency that buys printing on your behalf costing $85 net will increase the cost by 17.65 percent or $15 when billing you. Your bill from the agency for that printing will be for $100.

Some media use a dual rate card structure. If you are entitled to a "local rate" or "retail rate," remember that an agency cannot take a commission on these rates. Therefore, your agency, if it handles the placement of such advertising, probably will bill you the local or retail rate plus a 17.65 percent markup.

Advertising agencies located in one of the major markets, such as New York, Chicago, Atlanta, or San Francisco, often place advertising in out-of-town newspapers through a local representative of those papers. This gives them the convenience of a local pickup of materials and local service. However, since such media representatives operating in other market areas also receive a commission on advertising sold, the "general rate" or "national rate" may be considerably higher than the 15 percent differential that would cover the agency fee alone. A good rule to remember is that if you want to use advertising in local media, do not ever allow yourself to be billed at a "general rate" or a "national rate" unless an agency has placed the ad.

Many agencies bill on a fee basis because they do not want to tie their income to their ability to sell advertising to a client. Under the fee arrangement, the agency rebates to the client any commissions it may receive from media; the client pays net bills, and the agency receives its compensation in the form of a set fee.

One advantage of a fee arrangement is that the agency does not feel that if the client buys ads direct at the local rate, the agency is being cheated. Another is that the agency's income is based on a fixed charge for creative service, which enables it to recommend placement or discontinuance of advertising without prejudicing its own income.

Suppose you spend an average of $2,000 a month for advertising. An advertising agency might, through commissions, receive $300; artwork and markups on typesetting and printing might account for another $300. You and the agency might agree, on a six-month experimental basis, on a monthly fee of $600 for a specified number of service hours. If, during a month, you used more than the specified number of hours, the agency either would invoice you on a pro rata basis or else would deduct that number of hours from the next month.

Some advertising agencies work on a different kind of fee arrangement: the fee stands, regardless of the amount of work done during each month, and a mutual evaluation is made every six months.

Who Should Use an Agency?   Many yardsticks exist to determine whether an advertiser will profit or lose from a relationship with an advertising agency. One is this: If your advertising budget is $1,000 a month or more, chances are that an association with a competent, honest advertising agency will be profitable for you. Your promotional activities will get increased professional attention, and you will be exposed to moneysaving and dollar-stretching ideas.

However, do not expect a giant agency with billings of millions of dollars to handle your account unless it falls within a dollar range that can be profitable for them. Accounts billing below $25,000 annually should seek small agencies whose owner is directly involved in most of the accounts. Accounts billing between $25,000 and $100,000 a year should anticipate using an advertising agency whose staff may number from 10 to 20 people, since this size budget usually requires a reasonable amount of specialized personnel to handle. Accounts billing in excess of $100,000 ordinarily require a full-service agency with a complete range of specialized departments and strong staffing within those departments.

How to Select an Agency. Blindly choosing an advertising agency from the classified directory can be a serious mistake for both sides. The search for the right agency should be carefully and systematically handled.

One accepted procedure is for the businessman to prepare a question-naire with specific questions about various agencies' operations, their existing clientele, the range of services they offer internally, and their philosophies of service and compensation. From the answers, the client can determine which agencies are enthusiastic about his account and which of these may be satisfactory. He can make personal visits to the advertising shops to judge for himself their creative capabilities and their compatibil-ity with his own aims and goals. Or he can ask several promising adver-tising agencies, those whom he believes to be interested in his account and qualified to handle it, to submit proposals. In so doing, each agency will put its best foot forward, and a comparison of the presentations will give the advertiser an opportunity to evaluate each agency's thinking. He should not expect (especially on the industrial level) instant and thorough understanding of his product or service. He should look for the kind of people who will wear well in a business relationship, people with whom he feels he can work comfortably.

Unless the opportunity to acquire the account is important and likely, many agencies will not submit speculative campaigns or presentations. Some advertisers overcome this reluctance (which may eliminate the best-qualified agencies) by agreeing to pay for the presentation if the agency is not awarded the account.

Properly founded agency-client relationships can last for years, some-times for the life spans of both organizations. However, if a client feels that an agency is not functioning properly in his behalf, then that agency should be replaced.

CASHING IN ON TRENDS

"Holy carburetor, Batman! A new Ford for $2,088?" This headline, although not particularly inventive, made some sense in 1966, when the "Batman" television show burst into international prominence. In 1976, it would be as incomprehensible to most buyers as, "Yes, we have no bananas!"

Trends exist in terminology as well. "Rocket," "jet," and "atomic" all

This ad employs a design trend appropriate to both its product and its market. Would the same style be suitable for the advertiser of dishwashers or washing machines?

down to earth
...a shop offering
exclusively natural &
organic products...

33b seventh ave · 924-2710

the great organic food store

flamed briefly but now are burned out. "Showarama" and "Autorama" joined the many other "...ramas" for a brief period of popularity. "Magnetronic" and "Datatronic" were a few of the many "...tronics" fads.

These all were short-lived trends—fads. They had popularity; but an advertiser did not need to be particularly wise to know when to stop using them.

Each year it becomes more difficult to mount the type of total saturation assault that can produce a full-scale fad or popularity trend. During television's own novelty days, when viewers watched simply because the medium itself was new, it was possible to generate a Davy Crockett mania that lasted for more than a year. Today, such a promotion would be but one of many such projects all attempted at once.

Does it pay, then, to scour the newspapers, to sit with notebook in hand watching television, in hopes of unearthing something new that can be used for advertising purposes? It might, if you use it cleverly enough and soon enough—but most businessmen fear change and adopt the features of a trend only after its initial impact has been dissipated, thus giving their advertising only that weak "me too" look.

Trends involve ways of handling art and copy, as well as the actual tie-ins to particular customer fads. Using current trends can pay off—if they are used properly and quickly enough.

The Under-25s

Proof that statistics can be dangerous when misapplied is that frequently quoted statistic that half the population today is under 25 years of age. This has led advertisers to ignore the other half of the population (who have, among other benefits, the great bulk of buying power) and concentrate on the "young" words and phrases and on those situations and scenes with which this group supposedly identifies. (The overused word "relevant" describes this identification.)

The "young" group are supposedly the in-group. Yet, as an individual's buying power (and his age) increases, his desire to use the terminology of the "young" element usually declines. Youthfulness always has an appeal, but the fads of the young begin to seem sophomoric and trite.

Where "youth appeal" campaigns do indeed succeed is on the high school level, since high school students want to be identified with college students, and within the pages of underground newspapers, the readership of which trusts the advertisers simply because those advertisers have chosen to put their advertising in such publications. But an advertisement that is logical in an underground newspaper often would be only a curiosity if exposed to mass-circulation reactions. Its appeal and aptness would disappear, and novelty would be its only attraction for a larger and more varied audience.

Even using a teen-age or young adult advisory board is not the guaranteed way to reach the youth, assuming that they are an important market for you. Because such advisory boards often begin to take themselves very seriously, they may adopt words and terms that reveal the same forced and patronizing attitude that plagues older copywriters fighting to influence this market.

Writing for In-Groups

Perhaps surprisingly, even the proper and current clichés do not always catch the eyes of those who regularly may use them. An ad that loads itself with the current clichés of youth—"This is where it's at, baby" and "Hey, big daddy, try this in your crash pad!" and "Turn on with this groovy electric razor"—seldom has any credibility to the group at which it is aimed.

To what kind of advertising would such a group, or any other in-group, respond? For the trade and industrial advertiser, the question is academic. For the consumer advertiser and the manufacturer of products aimed at a particular group, the answer is that no proof has yet been found that any variation from the basic rules of headline writing and copywriting, those discussed in earlier chapters, is any improvement over straightforward, concise writing.

Readers identify and respond as individuals, not en masse. To assume that anyone in an age group, an ethnic group, or an economic group thinks and reacts in exactly the same way as everyone else in the group is oversimplifying human reactions. The well-told sales story, without any phoniness or in-group terminology, still attracts the largest number of those who can buy what you have to sell.

Therefore, you should use what appears to be a valid and alive trend—but don't overuse it, and don't let your advertising become enslaved by it.

Trends in Graphics

More definite stylistic changes are seen in advertising art than in copy, probably because artists are more constantly in search of change. In one recent 3-year period, modern "block" art yielded to psychedelic art, which yielded to a comic book style, which yielded to a 1920s cartoon style.

Never assume that there is a wholesale bandwagon acceptance of trends in art. Instead, there is an overall long-range evolution of style both in layout and in illustration. This can be seen by examining a series of annual catalogs, say the Sears, Roebuck catalogs, for a period of 20 years or so. There is not that much difference obvious from one edition to the next—but a tremendous difference can be noted by comparing one catalog with another issued 20 years later.

Such a comparison also would underscore the evolution that has taken place in typefaces. The ornateness that characterized early advertising typography has been replaced by a more readable, cleaner-lined group of typefaces. The baroque has been abandoned and the functional has been adopted. This evolution in typography almost directly parallels changes in architecture, to which it is related.

MARKET RESEARCH

All advertising and sales promotion is intended to help achieve one or both of two goals: to generate sales and/or to create and maintain an image. In a way, the second goal is another facet of the first, for by creating and maintaining a specific image a marketer hopes to generate more sales.

To reach these goals, a businessman should know who his customers are and which of the products and services he can offer they will want to buy and in what amounts. Only when he knows this information can he set a specific sales goal, backed up by a specific amount and kind of inventory and promoted by a specific amount and kind of advertising and sales promotion efforts.

Compiling this information is the job of market research.

Market research used to be a once-a-year chore. When the time came to plan next year's operations, a businessman would sit down with his books, check his past sales, think about the state of the market, and make a rough guess about what the next year could be like. Some businessmen still use this kind of guesswork as the basis for their plans, but they are not among the more successful businessmen.

Today's successful marketers, small and large alike, know that market research is a continuing job and that collecting and analyzing market information is the only way to build up good plans for the future. No matter what the size of a business, if that business shows a firm and steady growth the businessman probably uses some system of market research. A large marketer may have a computer system full of facts and programs, while a small marketer may rely on a notebook and a filing cabinet, but both have worked out the systems they need.

The necessary information can come from both inside and outside the company. Most marketers use both sources. Many of the figures collected as a normal part of bookkeeping routine are useful in a market research program; other data can be collected from a variety of outside sources.

Internal Sources

Customer information can be useful; any retail store with a charge account setup has such information in its accounts receivable files. Who are the marketer's customers? What are they like? This means identifying customers by demographics: age, income, type and location of home, profession, sex, ethnic background, special interests. Such information not only helps the retailer choose the merchandise that will satisfy those customers but also helps him promote that merchandise in the media important to those customers and in the terms those customers understand.

Research Projects

When such information is not already in the files, it is possible to run your own research project. An example might be a project set up to choose the name of a fish-and-chips carry-out restaurant that you are considering opening. Which name would have the most appeal: "Limey's," "Davy Jones's Locker," or " 'Er Majesty's Pantry"? One approach to an answer is to station a bright student outside an existing fish-and-chips location (or hire a trained researcher to do the job, for trained interviewers often can collect more variety and less bias in data). Have the interviewer ask those leaving the restaurant to check their preference among a list of five names, the three you liked best and two others chosen as controls. No matter what you learn, you will have more valid data to use than your own guesswork could ever produce.

This primitive research project actually is, in miniature, the manner in which many major market research activities are mounted. While one should not become bogged down in research that proves of little value to him, it is far worse to charge blindly into marketing with neither background nor a sense of public opinion.

To the businessman with a nonretail marketing problem, research may be equally important. Since his prospective customers probably are not located in a single geographic area, he may have to gather information by mail. The two overriding questions should be whether or not the information being sought is actually available—and, if so, whether it will be of value in advertising and sales promotion.

External Sources

Never restrict yourself to data collected only by or within your own organization. By doing this, you eliminate the important outside sources that can tell you what is happening not only in the marketplace in general but also in your particular field of interest in that marketplace. Some information, purchased from a company that specializes in market research, can be expensive. However, much free information is available.

Your suppliers, for instance, are a rich source of facts and ideas about trends in your field. They will be delighted to share this information with you, because it should help you to sell more of their products. Often your suppliers and vendors will send out the results of their market research both free and unsolicited, and nearly always a supplier will try to answer carefully any specific questions his own customers may ask him. While those who sell to you can give you a much broader view of the whole field than you could learn from your own records, there is just one warning about such information: Since a vendor wants to encourage the sales of his own products, regardless of market trends, he may tend to play down any adverse trend for his particular kind of product and play up the data that indicates good sales for him.

Trade associations are another source of useful information. Most trade associations collect statistics within their particular fields and make those statistics available to their members at a nominal fee. These statistics are unbiased in that they represent the collective experiences of the members of the association; however, they sometimes are biased, depending upon the size and scope of the membership, in that they usually reflect only the experience of those companies who are members and who submitted information that would make the statistics questionable as representative of the entire industry.

In order to benefit their members, trade associations constantly compile information that can be valuable to those on the perimeter of the industry. Because marketing is the core of any business, inevitably much of this information reflects on merchandising methods. Associations also sponsor studies that may provide direct answers to the problems of marketing, since such problems are usually industrywide. For example, a trade association may publish for its members a manual about proper use of Yellow Pages advertising or localized public relations or new markets, or it may distribute informative pamphlets containing condensations of speeches and papers delivered at meetings and conventions.

Trade publications are another good source of data. Even the demographic surveys taken by a publication are helpful. Suppose, for instance, that you wanted to reach the buyers of computer components. Should you advertise in *Data Processing* or in *Data Product News*? The answer is simple if you know where to obtain the facts you need (and space salesmen, always anxious to sell, are not always the most reliable source of accurate information). An easy reference source for such information is the readership breakdown that is part of the publication's listing in the Standard Rate and Data volume, *Business Publication Rates and Data*, in which both the aforementioned magazines and all others of any consequence to advertisers in the field are listed.

As another example, major newspapers maintain research departments that sometimes look for projects to undertake. As the franchisor of a fried chicken carry-out, you might convince the newspaper's research staff to determine what your competitive image is, which fast-food franchise seems to be growing fastest in the area, whose advertising seems to have the most impact, and whose fried chicken is regarded as superior.

There is considerable information around, both for the taking and for the buying. But before becoming so immersed in the acquisition of background information that the original purpose is blunted, keep in mind this point: Market research is a means, not an end. The information collected and analyzed is to be put to use in your planning. Never let yourself become so fascinated by the collection of information that you forget that the reason you have collected data is to use it.

Facts about circulation growth

Subscribers, many for long terms, account for virtually all (98.6%) of Organic Gardening's circulation. Most subscriptions come in by word-of-mouth recommendations or responses to full-price mail appeals. Subscriptions are not sold by agents or with cut-price gimmicks.

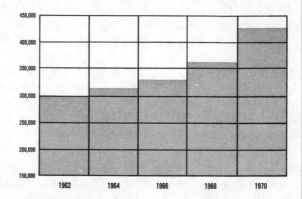

Facts about duplication

Subscribers were asked to check other gardening magazines they read regularly. As the data shows, neither of the other 2 major magazines in the field has made much of an impact on Organic Gardening's audience.

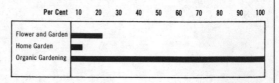

Facts about cost-per-thousand

Data taken from Standard Rate & Data.

Flower and Garden	$4.15
Home Garden	$6.05
Organic Gardening	$3.36

Courtesy of **Organic Gardening**

Publications often attract advertisers by supplying them with information on circulation, editorial content, readership demographics, and cost. This is one sheet of a promotion brochure for Organic Gardening *magazine.*

A PROGRAM OF READING

Too many professionals in the advertising world believe that the only publications that will give them a rounded view of their profession are the advertising publications: *Advertising Age, Industrial Marketing, Advertising and Sales Promotion,* and *Marketing Communications,* among them.

These publications do discuss, literately and authoritatively, the main trends in advertising. But they are geared primarily to the big-budget advertisers, and campaigns are judged in comparison with each other, not as individual successes or failures.

The businessman who wants to keep up with changing trends and terminology should read these publications. But he also should read widely in two other groups: trade publications and general publications.

The dangers of reading only within a vertical field can be recognized when one thinks of the people he himself knows who can discuss only the professions in which they find themselves. Such people are inevitably dull, uninformed, and boring. Add to this the dimension required for advertising and sales promotion—the requirement of communications—and it becomes clear that advertising reflecting only a one-faceted source of information will itself be dull, uninformed, and boring.

Broadening one's base of friendships also helps one to learn to communicate with more people. Those who know only a small group of friends often are the same persons who read little outside of their field.

Trade Publications

Must reading are the trade publications within the professional, commercial, or industrial fields that touch your area of business in any way. Reading these publications will keep your thinking current. As you read, clip advertisements that impress you—and clip the advertising of any of your competitors. If yours is a retail or consumer business, you can benefit from the trade advertising of the products you sell, because such ads will give you more information about merchandising trends and techniques.

In addition, almost every issue of every trade magazine has in its editorial content marketing information that can be valuable to you. Articles may be staff-written or they may be written by outside sources; however, they usually are authoritative, or they would not be given space in the publication. Often, through either personal interviews or mailed questionnaires, information has been compiled that can be of great value to the serious advertiser trying to pinpoint his market or find better ways of selling to that market.

General Publications

Everyone who has anything to do with marketing in general and with advertising and sales promotion in particular constantly should try to broaden his field of knowledge in a variety of subjects. *Mad* magazine can be as important as *Time* or *Newsweek*, if *Mad* is likely to be read by any of your customers. It obviously will not be a source of marketing information and news, but it will be a source of current thinking.

The businessman who reads the fashion pages of his newspaper is not being feminine, and the woman who reads the sports pages is not being masculine; both are broadening their backgrounds of general information. Such information can be useful when one has the job of transmitting information in terms of the background of a particular target customer rather than in one's own terms of experience.

Every library has books that penetrate deeply into each of the areas of marketing, communications, and sales promotion. Reading one of these books each month is no major chore—and within a short time, the technical background you will have built up will surprise the time and space salesmen who call on you.

No subject should be a complete mystery to you—not if it may be important to your communication with those who might buy what you have to sell or may help you in your operations more efficiently and effectively.

One of the best procedures anyone in communications can follow is to clip, file, and occasionally reread any article or ad that seems worth the trouble. No, don't clip those library books—but if something seems particularly useful, you probably could photocopy it right at the library.

If you set up a clipping file, remember to read the material before filing it—and then remember to reread it occasionally. Too many businessmen who begin to clip interesting pieces soon file them automatically and never look at them again.

The point of reading both inside and outside your profession is to avoid stagnation. By broadening your base of knowledge, you are less likely to misinterpret a trend, less likely to substitute humor for message, and less likely to assume that doing what the giants do is always correct.

BUDGETING

Company A spent $10,000 on advertising and sales promotion and had sales of $300,000. Company B spent $10,000 on advertising and sales promotion during the same period and had sales of $250,000. Which campaign was the most successful?

The answer? We need more information to judge.

The statistics seem plain: Each dollar that Company A spent on advertising and sales promotion earned the company $30 in sales, while each dollar that Company B spent on advertising and sales promotion earned the company $25 in sales. Assuming that all other expenses per dollar of sales were the same for both companies, it would seem that Company A had put on the more successful campaign.

However, what if Company A, for the same expenditure in advertising and sales promotion, had had sales of $350,000 the year before—and what if Company B had just entered the market and, in its first year, had surpassed ten other brands whose expenditures were almost as high and had obviously eaten into Company A's sales? Then the answer changes—just one of the ways in which it could change.

A budget should not be absolute in itself. It should be geared to something: sales, image, product introduction, market expansion, meeting competition. Company A's expenditures in advertising and sales promotion may have been planned simply in terms of a sales goal; Company B's budget may have included appropriations gauged to cover product introduction, market expansion, and meeting preexisting competition.

Even after a budget is planned, it must be flexible. As time and the campaign progress, the budget must be continually evaluated and adjusted to cover unexpected changes that may have taken place in the market.

A budget must be planned in advance; but once planned, no budget should ever be rigid and unchanging, and no budget should ever allocate all the available resources. There should always be room for adjustment and changes, so that the company can meet unexpected situations and take advantage of unexpected opportunities.

Importance of Planning

Those who believe that a professional knowledge of advertising is limited to the cleverly turned phrase and the startling headline are usually those who do not or will not take the time to plan the proper budget to

April 1, 19--

MARY LESTER FABRICS PROMOTION

1.   Budget --- $15,000.   Three-week period.

We recommend use of saturation radio, community newspapers, and metropolitan newspapers. Budget is insufficient for significant television coverage.

    a. Radio:

        WGN --- this is the class-mass station. Recommend
        $1,300 weekly for 3 weeks. This will include Wally
        Phillips (strongest on-the-air Chicago audience)
        plus substantial daytime coverage. $ 3,900

        WBBM --- this is the "class" audience that will
        respond to the new surge of do-it-yourself sewing.
        Recommend $1,000 weekly saturation 9-word
        (expandable) commercials for 3 weeks.   3,000

        WJJD --- this is the country and western station.
        Audience should be prime for this client. Station
        is No. 4 in daytime ratings. Recommend $500 weekly
        for 3 weeks.   1,500

    b. Community newspapers:

        Lerner-Life papers --- these dominate the area in
        which the new store will open. Standard page format
        means that no variation from normal column-width is
        required. Recommend $500 weekly for 3 weeks.   1,500

    c. Metropolitan newspapers:

        Chicago Sun-Times --- strong middle-income circulation.
        Should provide best citywide coverage for this client.
        Recommend Sunday and Thursday coverage, $400 weekly for
        3 weeks.   1,200

        Chicago Tribune --- needed for total citywide coverage.
        Sunday and Thursday coverage can be centered around
        multiple small--space ads in the same issue. Recommend
        $300 weekly for 3 weeks.   900

    d. Production, type, and art.   1,000

    e. Public relations, publicity, and creative.   2,000
                                                                        ——————
                                                       Total $15,000

Do you think that this advertising and sales promotion budget reflects carefully planning?

implement the bright ideas. By properly planning an advertising and sales promotion budget, a businessman not only can avoid the unpleasant surprises that can accompany invoices for work that has been ordered haphazardly but also strongly increase his chances of reaching his marketing goals.

Major Budget Methods

"How do I know how much to spend to get my money's worth?" asks the businessman. There are three major methods used to determine the budget for advertising and sales promotion: goal-achievement, percentage-of-sales, and meet-the-competition.

Goal-Achievement Method. Businessmen who use this method budget according to the amount needed to get the job done—or achieve their goals. Of the three methods, goal achievement is usually the best, provided that the decisions are made professionally, on the basis of market information and research, and not emotionally. It is the worst method if the marketer lets emotions, pipedreams, or guesswork prevail.

Major companies almost universally use market research to set the budget. As discussed earlier, by collecting and analyzing sales data and other kinds of market information, sales trends can be forecast, variables considered, and a logical and dispassionate conclusion reached about the goals to be set for the coming year.

The larger marketer often uses computer techniques in this research, but the smaller marketer can hand-carve this important market information from his own records and from outside sources. Yet too few businessmen running smaller operations take the trouble. Frequently the smaller businessman does more guesswork than spadework, and the budget projection is influenced too strongly by what happened last week or last month instead of long-range thinking.

In order to determine the amount required to get the job done, this is the information you must have, in addition to the kind of information discussed in the market research section:

- What sales do you project?

- Do you need sales leads?

- Do you need additional distributors?

- What resources—money, time, equipment—will be needed to reach each goal you set?

From previous experience, for example, you might know that your moving and storage company spends an average of $50 in advertising and sales promotion for each customer it serves. If your company can operate profitably at this figure and if your capacity is double the number of customers you have had, your approach to setting a budget figure might be to double the previous expenditure.

And you might then find that the method is invalid simply because you are oversaturating one particular market. The dollars may be right but the figuring is wrong; the solution may lie elsewhere. For instance, perhaps you should invest in other advertising media that reach a different group of prospects, or perhaps you should merchandise a different aspect of your business from the one you have been emphasizing.

When planning a budget, one should consider more than the cost of the advertising and sales promotion alone. He must be sure he has the capability of handling additional volume, of expanding into other areas of activity, or of developing new geographical markets if any of these is one of his goals. Otherwise, his advertising and sales promotion may produce leads, but he will be unable to turn those leads into sales.

Percentage-of-Sales Method. Although in practice the second method of determining budget, allocating a flat percentage of total sales or business volume, is used at least as often as the first method, it can have one obvious drawback: If the budget is based on accomplished sales, rather than logically anticipated sales, then to some extent the budget is looking backward, not forward.

Businessmen using this method are forced to cut the budget when sales figures drop—and this may be exactly the wrong direction in which to move. Lagging sales thus are given no impetus or boost but instead are given additional discouragement.

What happens is that results dictate motivation, in a situation in which the motivation should dictate results. Instead of recognizing that advertising brings sales, this philosophy suggests that sales create advertising. Strict adoption of this method of budget allocation divorces advertising from the other aspects of marketing.

A variation of the percentage-of-sales method is the dollar-per-unit method, which builds budgets by allocating a specific number of dollars for each unit sold. For example, a manufacturer of automobiles will spend (and, additionally, allow his dealers to spend) a flat number of dollars for each car sold. A brewer will spend so many dollars per barrel produced and sold.

Much cooperative advertising is figured on the basis of dollars per unit. A local appliance dealer will be allowed $15 by the manufacturer for each television set he buys from that manufacturer, or he may be allowed a cash amount up to 4 or 5 percent of his total purchases from that manufacturer, to spend on advertising in his local market. (Under the terms of most cooperative advertising agreements, the local dealer must match the allowance dollar for dollar).

Cooperative advertising figured on this basis, although consistent with the rules laid down in the Robinson-Patman Act, fails to recognize that the need to advertise differs from situation to situation. Dealers use their cooperative advertising allowances because they are there, not because they have value. And they use the advertising materials sent by the manufacturer—newspaper mats, radio continuity, or even open-end television commercials—because these are available, when in fact they may have better methods of local merchandising that they use in noncooperative advertising situations.

Huge retailers may well regard cooperative advertising as the cornerstone of their ad budgets. For example, more than 50 percent of E.J. Korvette's metropolitan New York budget is paid for by suppliers. Some retailers, through marked-up production costs and media rebates, collect more co-op money than they spend—a disservice to this valuable method of budget-stretching.

Meet-the-Competition Method. The third method, budgeting according to what the competition is doing, is the least scientific and the most uncertain of all. Not only does the marketer let his competitor dictate his budget, but the marketer is always one step behind his competitor. This is a bit like a chess game in which you in turn move exactly the same man your opponent has moved; by doing this, you can checkmate your opponent—one move after he has checkmated you.

It should be recognized that no matter how competitive a marketplace is, and no matter how similar the product or service offered by two companies is, the marketing problems and the overall objectives of those two companies never are identical. Proof of the deficiency of this method is that any businessman considers that he is a step ahead if his principal competitor copies his budget and his media selection. Nevertheless, too many decide, "If he's advertising there, maybe we'd better be in there, too!"

Other Budget Methods

Sometimes a company discards all three major methods of budget determination in favor of a how-much-can-I-afford method, or perhaps an autocratic method, or a cost-per-lead method. The first is used too frequently by beginning marketers; the second often is a favorite of large one-man-run and very conservative companies; the third can be useful in some forms of business.

How-Much-Can-I-Afford Method. Since advertising and sales promotion too often are the first expenditures to be eliminated when dollars are tight, the how-much-can-I-afford method is likely to result in too small a budget to start and cuts in that budget as time goes on. Few beginning marketers, faced with a situation in which the total number of dollars available for any marketing purpose is dictated in advance, will provide enough funds for advertising and sales promotion. They act more like gamblers than businessmen investing in the future.

Because of this, a number of franchisors require their new franchisees to allocate a specific amount for advertising the first year of business, recognizing that otherwise the franchisee may feel he cannot afford advertising at all that first troublesome year. By building the expenditure into a required budget, the parent company does its best to get the franchisee off to a good start.

The Autocratic Method. Another method results in a dictated statement from top management saying, "We are allocating so-and-so many dollars for advertising and sales promotion this year." The amount is arbitrarily determined. Should the edict be based on research, the terminology would no longer apply, because a calculation based on any kind of logical market research would represent one of the first two major methods.

This is a method occasionally used by older companies that have

enjoyed, are enjoying, and expect to continue to enjoy a steady business—
and that usually are privately owned by an individual or a family.

Cost-per-Lead Method. The easiest and, for some companies, often the
most foolproof method of determining budget is the cost-per-lead method.
This is an effective technique for the businessman whose volume depends
upon names of prospects obtained by advertising.

Such businesses—schools, direct selling organizations, home improvement sales companies, insurance brokers, franchise sales companies, and
the like—can judge the effectiveness of their advertising by the number of
qualified leads (pronounced "leeds," not "leds") that their advertising
produces. Many such companies, basing their success on a percentage of
lead conversions, determine at what point the cost of leads is profitable
and will advertise anywhere and in any way so long as this cost per lead
remains in line with the budget.

For example, a company selling beer coolers for home use may know
that its salesmen will close one of every four legitimate leads. The company's bookkeeping dictates that a maximum of $35 per $100 unit can be
spent, including sales commission, if the company is to be operated
profitably. If the salesman gets a 20 percent commission, or $20, per unit
sold, this leaves $15 per unit for advertising. And since the average closure
rate is one in four, this means that advertising must produce four leads for
$15—$3.75 per lead.

This company will budget, therefore, any advertising—newspaper, radio,
television, direct mail, telephone, or personal contact—that can be bought,
provided it produces leads that cost no more than $3.75 each and that are
of a quality comparable to those already being worked by the salesmen.
(The businessman must analyze leads carefully to determine their source,
especially if he advertises in several media.)

A LOOK TO THE FUTURE

There no longer is any such thing in communications as a "startling
development." Instant communication has become so taken for granted
that there is little wonder left in its particular world. Even those who were
there are hard pressed to remember their awe as, in 1948, they stared at
their three-inch or seven-inch black-and-white television screens and

watched a television show that actually was seen up and down the East Coast and as far west as Chicago all at the same time.

While nothing may seem startling, there is much that is excitingly new—new in that these tools and techniques are only beginning to be used and, when used more widely, probably will change many facets of the world of advertising and sales promotion perhaps together with the principles of communications themselves.

New Tools

New techniques and new media are reported in the trade press almost monthly. Some of the most promising include videocassettes, videofax, and new developments in pay TV, closed-circuit TV, and CATV.

Videocassettes. The miniature tape cassette, which first reached widespread use and popularity in the late 1960s, may be replaced or joined by a film or videotape cassette of equal handiness. Certainly videocassettes should become an important factor both in entertainment and in instruction, but whether this will be a factor in advertising or sales promotion is uncertain.

One obvious use of videocassettes for advertising and sales promotion is the development of the "sponsored" entertainment cassette. In such a circumstance, a sponsor prepares a videocassette that might, if consumer-oriented, contain entertainment, or if business-oriented, contain instruction. Together with the information on the videocassette (or perhaps subtly interwoven with it) is a commercial message.

Videofax. The inevitable increase in the amount of leisure time should mean a continuing rise in the curve of listenership, viewership, and readership. Experiments already are well advanced concerning such novelties as reproduction of the day's newspaper on a console in the home.

The machinery for "videofax" has been available for years. It parallels the procedures whereby wirephotos are transmitted by the wire services and, were this method of communication to become popular, sophistication of existing hardware should be simple. Some stores already are conducting on a more than experimental basis an approach to purchasing through a combination of wares shown on closed-circuit television and computerized order cards that may activate a telephone signal.

Pay TV. The advocates of pay television say that its rise is inevitable. Part of the sales argument made by pay TV's proponents is that this medium will be free from advertising. Yet one wonders whether anyone in control of a communications medium can resist the natural urge to capitalize on the huge audience that can be anticipated for an exclusive showing of a major entertainment or sports event.

Closed-Circuit TV. Heavyweight championship fights, which so far have represented the largest amounts of dollars generated by closed-circuit television, have themselves shown the slow inching toward the inclusion of commercial messages; the differences between attending a closed-circuit event in a theatre or in a living room is one of locale, not of procedure.

CATV. CATV (Community Antenna Television) operators must, under an order by the Federal Communications Commission, originate programming. Programming includes commercials—and since many CATV installations have limited subscription, they represent a good test market.

Some commercial sources have offered to supply the programming for the CATV operators in exchange for use of commercial time within those programs; this is the same principle of bartered time that has been something of a specialty in normal commercial television, in which companies trade programs for minutes of commercial time, then sell that time at prices below the station's normal rate to any and all who are willing to buy it.

Candor: Blessing or Curse?

It was not until the 1950s that brassieres were considered acceptable products for television exposure. Hemorrhoid compounds were unmentionable until the late 1950s. But as the walls began to tumble in the late 1960s, even products for feminine hygiene were sold by intensive and reasonably explicit television advertising with hardly a murmur from critics.

As advertising entered the 1970s, hard liquor still was barred from broadcast advertising. A mild experiment by Schenley in the 1940s had resulted in enormous pressure being brought to ban such advertising. But it is possible that whiskey advertising, which is visible constantly in other media, may slide quietly into broadcast media during this period of permissiveness.

Cigarette advertising, on the other hand, has a more uncertain future. In addition to the broadcast media ban, such august publications as *The Reader's Digest* announced their own rejection of advertising for cigarettes. As a result, tobacco companies tend to advertise based on media acceptance of their advertising; they also sponsor sports events as a means of achieving editorial coverage.

Certainly we can expect advertising to become more candid in the upcoming years. If the permissive society stays with us, no subject will be taboo—which will mean that concerned parents will have to exercise as much vigilance over their children's television viewing and the parts of the newspaper they read as they have in past years over which motion pictures the children have been allowed to see.

Changes in Magazines

Many authorities in the magazine field claim that the near future will see massive changes in the frequency of issuance. For example, magazines with a sports format might bunch issues in months in which there is much major sports activity and issue no magazines in lean months.

Obviously, one trend is towards greater usage of specific segments of a magazine's circulation. In addition to geographic breakdowns in which an advertiser will be able to pinpoint his advertising to specific ZIP codes, demographic breakdowns are becoming available in a wide range of magazines, trade as well as consumer. For example, one will be able to reach the doctors or schoolteachers or business executives or students or purchasing agents or plant managers who represent a segment of the readership of a particular magazine.

And the publications themselves may well divide their issues, producing editions tailored for the various age, ethnic, and economic groups that comprise their total readership. The subscriber to a magazine may be asked to indicate which edition he wants to receive.

Automated Typography

Certainly one can anticipate improvements in the automation of the business of preparing advertisements, and these improvements are closer than speculation might indicate.

Computerized typesetting already is a fact. Typewriter-keyboard type-setting is a fact. Neither has reached into areas of advertising. In the case of typesetting by computer, a number of national magazines already use punched tape or electronic signals to set type simultaneously in several printing plants. But the multiplicity of typefaces and the absence of standardization of column widths or point sizes has meant that the only moneysavers available to the advertiser have been cold type, Varitype, and the IBM typesetter.

The IBM typesetter is limited both in typefaces and in type sizes. It can be expected that as acceptance and production of these units grow, adaptations will be made available which will set larger sizes. And, too, a greater variety of typefaces with more pleasing, artistic designs must be marketed if this technique is to reach its potential as an advertising tool.

Outdoor and Transit Advertising

The current triangular, changing outdoor signs, which make possible the use of a single sign for three separate messages, already have been combined with electronic signs that add additional impact to the change from

Courtesy of Metromedia Transit Advertising

A recent concept in transit advertising is the use of all of the interior advertising space by one advertiser. This increases impact and reader involvement.

one message to the next. For example, a food company that has many products may use the sign for ice cream, bread, and pickles. As each of these three messages rotates into position, a flashing strip below the sign adds a written message, timed to change as the sign itself changes.

Projected signs are another novelty for which commercial possibilities are blossoming into reality. The side of any building becomes the site of a sign, with none of the cost of painting, repainting, stenciling, and changing. Instead, a message is projected from another installation, using a high-powered xenon or arc lamp for an intense image.

Transit advertising also is undergoing modernization. In addition to the rear-illuminated plastic signs that have replaced the old cardboard ones, pilot installations of projected motion picture, slide, and television images have added new life and attraction value to this form of advertising. Such developments have direct media results as well: it becomes possible to buy transit advertising to reach a more pinpointed audience—for example, the morning commuters, the between-rush-hour shoppers, the evening riders, all with a different message or even a different advertiser.

Montreal's subway has another innovation. Through photoelectric cells, the window lights of a passing train activate a series of illuminated frames that form a total sequence as the train travels through its tunnel.

GETTING YOUR MONEY'S WORTH

The average housewife is exposed to up to 2,000 advertising messages a day. The competitive nature of the cries for attention is why so much time and money are spent working out ways of increasing the ability of one message to dominate another.

As we move toward a four-day workweek, everyone will have more time to be exposed to and react to advertising messages. Armed only with the knowledge of advertising and sales promotion techniques and of motivation that existed in 1900, an advertising expert could not hope to compete today. He would represent a time and a dimension of narrow vistas and limited media selectivity, and he would depend upon an "announcement" type of advertising in an era in which such advertising would be not only out of date but also too weak to compete.

In exactly the same way, today's expert will not be able to compete tomorrow—unless he keeps up with new trends and techniques.

Advertising and sales promotion are complex, dynamic, and competitive, and no one can be totally expert in every phase of the field. This is why alertness and constant study will pay off in dollars.

Ways of Failing

There are ten types of advertisers who consistently fail to get their money's worth from their advertising and who usually are unable to recognize the reasons why. Here is a list of losers:

1. The advertiser who falls in love with his own ideas and refuses outside counsel.

2. The advertiser who believes that a headline with a pun is superior to a headline with information.

3. The advertiser who is so graphics-oriented that message is secondary to beauty in his ads.

4. The advertiser who uses his child's artwork, his wife's picture, and a "see what a nice boy I am, Mom?" attitude as his advertising.

5. The advertiser who is subject to the high-pressure sales pitch of the nearest time or space salesman.

6. The advertiser who dismisses all time and space salesmen as selfserving.

7. The advertiser who buys advertising only in publications he himself likes.

8. The advertiser who insists on changing his ad with every insertion, regardless of the success of the current ad.

9. The advertiser who waits for his competition to make a move before he moves himself.

10. The advertiser who uses his advertising to impress the reader with his knowledge of big words.

Ways of Succeeding

"Why do people buy?" This question should be in the mind of anyone in the marketplace each time he considers his advertising and sales promotion. There is no single answer because the field itself is fluid and changing. Selling is a peculiar blend of economics, sociology, and psychology. Reasons for buying change, not only over an extended period but also overnight.

The successful marketer listens to his customers' conversations; he scouts the competition; he keeps up with innovations and refuses to stand still with the ideas he used 20 years before.

The Ultimate Rule. If there is any single rule that should dominate the thinking of anyone spending money on advertising and sales promotion, it is:

Watch every dollar.

This demands that the businessman who is not a full-time advertising expert nevertheless be a constant student of this craft. You never will know that you are getting your dollar's worth unless you check the results of your campaigns just as carefully as you planned those campaigns in the first place. Over a surprisingly short period, you can chart your promotion's effectiveness and learn more about the subtler aspects of psychological appeals than you ever thought existed. And remember that checking results, like planning, is a continuing job.

Learn what does the job for you—and keep learning.

NOW, APPLY WHAT YOU'VE LEARNED

Test your ability to use all the tools, recognize trends, and get your money's worth in advertising and sales promotion, based on the information in this chapter.

1. Prepare a list of questions to be answered by four advertising agencies that you invite to solicit your machine tool account, which bills $75,000 a year in trade media, direct mail, and trade shows. Answers to the questions should tell you if the agencies are qualified and interested.

2. You operate a chain of six dry-cleaning stores. Using all available information from two local radio stations, write an evaluation that indicates which station you would use and why.

3. You are a soft drink bottler whose $50,000 budget is spent almost entirely on television. Are you better off dealing direct or using an advertising agency? Write a 500-word analysis explaining your point of view.

4. For any locally advertised consumer product, obtain some professional research information that is of value in marketing; then, using that information, plan a basic campaign idea.

5. Make a list of ten phrases currently in use because of fads, television comedians, or local jokes. Find an ad that uses one of these as a headline.

6. Make a similar list of ten phrases that may have been current one to ten years ago but which are no longer in common use.

7. Your company makes "Luau" Soy Sauce. First, learn the uses of soy sauce; then write two ads, one for the under-25 readership and one for the over-25 readership.

8. You manufacture eyeglasses and sunglasses. Last year, with a volume of $200,000, you spent $20,000 on advertising and netted $20,000. Your advertising was divided as follows: $10,000 newspapers; $5,000 direct mail; $2,000 premiums;

$3,000 miscellaneous. This year, you want to expand. Using the budget-determining method based on the amount needed to get the job done, make up this year's budget. Then, in a few paragraphs, justify that budget and point out the pitfalls that might be in it and what you will do if after a month or two your new budget does not seem to work.

9. You sell dance lessons. The cost of your business operation is such that you can spend $10 for each live lead. Make up a one-month budget of $5,000, outlining with each media buy why you believe that leads can be generated for a cost below $10.

10. Find at least one example of any of the new devices and techniques described in this chapter.